Progressive Relaxation Training
A Manual for the Helping Professions

Douglas A. Bernstein, Ph.D.

Thomas D. Borkovec, Ph.D.

Foreword by
Leonard P. Ullmann

RESEARCH PRESS
2612 North Mattis Avenue · Champaign, Illinois 61820

ISBN 0-87822-104-2

15 14 13 12   86 87 88 89 90

Cover Design / Claudette Rodgers

This book is dedicated to the memory of Morris Belkin.

Contents

Foreword

Often people come to therapists knowing what they should be doing, but not how to accomplish their goals. In particular, many people know they should "relax" but, as with much of behavior therapy with intelligent adults, the problem becomes how to accomplish the task, and it is in this context that this volume offers its first contribution to the working clinician.

As one who has both written and taught in this field, I greatly appreciate and admire this book's complete and careful coverage of topics. Both the organization and the quality of communication are superb; but the ease of reading should not cause the reader to ignore an important warning given by the authors: every sentence carries an important message. While some general meaning may be obtained by skimming, good clinical usage of this manual demands careful study of the entire book. The volume is filled with information based on actual clinical experience.

Relaxation procedures may be used, as is described in this volume, as an end in themselves or as a part of more complicated procedures such as systematic desensitization. In either case, it is the therapist's and the research worker's responsibility to be thoroughly competent in the technique. There are many examples, in both case work and research, of people who have carelessly evaluated new procedures, only to expose their own slipshod procedures and indifference to excellence. Such work is inexcusable, especially now that this manual is available. The worker now need not create his own program but has a careful and complete source from which he may proceed. A good technique should transcend individual differences in application and there is no reason why any therapist should not improve his skills as a result of a study of this work.

Technique, however, can never replace thoughtfulness, sensitivity, and flexibility. One of the interesting features of this book is the picture of the therapist that it presents. The therapist is poised, competent, and has a sense of humor; he is very much attuned to the client and ready to adjust his procedures on the basis of the client's responses.

The client, in turn, is viewed as an intelligent, coping person. There is a constant emphasis on the client making use of a technique rather than on his being a passive person. Relaxation may produce specific helpful physiological effects. It may be used both within the therapy situation, as during systematic desensitization or interviewing, or it may be used in the extra-therapy environment as a response with which to deal with stressful situations. (The force of reality is stronger than the effect of any image used in systematic desensitization and, as long as the level of tension is reduced, learning in actual situations—*in vivo* desensitization—may also take place.) In addition, having the response of relaxation, even if it serves only as a distraction, may help the person deal more effectively at an operant level with the situation, and this success may in turn reduce future reluctance, avoidance, or irrelevant arousal.

Sensitivity to one's own bodily feelings is a topic of growing interest to both the profession and the general public. It is very easy to provide situations that increase or decrease physiological arousal. The manual offers something more constructive: not only a way of discriminating levels of arousal or tension, but also a way of putting such knowledge to use. Once such learning has been found valuable in coping with extra-therapy situations, we may expect that the quest will continue in a task-relevant manner rather than in a random sensational fashion.

The authors state in a number of different contexts that relaxation is not a panacea. There are situations in which tension and caution are realistic responses, and there are other situations in which the problem is not physiological arousal but a lack of some academic, physical, or social skill, and frequently relaxation procedures may facilitate further diagnostic efforts. Once a person has learned to attend to bodily responses, he may learn to view such responses as antecedents to further acts. Situations in which well-learned typical relaxation responses fail are ones to which special attention should be given. The person can change a source of upsetting stimuli, i.e., his physiological responses, to a genuine help and guide, a system that alerts him to the need for further learning. We should not aim for a person devoid of tension; our ideal should be a comfortable person alert to both his internal and external environments. We try to help people deal with their environments actively and effectively. Within this context, relaxation is not only an end, but, once mastered, also a means.

The goals for the client are the goals for the therapist. The present volume provides a method to use and to integrate into a full therapy program. It provides a means, and not an end in itself, not a replacement for knowledge, creativity, and sensitivity. By providing such a clearly written, complete, and balanced book, Douglas Bernstein and Thomas Borkovec have provided an invaluable aid for anyone involved in either research or practice. Just as the client may find relaxation both an end and a means to additional goals, so the therapist will find that this book provides both information which is immediately useful *and* a method to be integrated with future creative developments.

Leonard P. Ullmann

The authors wish to acknowledge the helpful comments provided by Dr. Gordon Paul early in preparation of the manuscript for this book, as well as the expert assistance of Dr. Donald T. Shannon who made the recording which accompanies it. The editorial skills of Phyllis Holmen, Mary Borkovec, and Sue Robinson, along with the research assistance of Kathy Singerman, are also gratefully acknowledged.

1 Introduction

Modern psychotherapy is on a new frontier in the development and application of a wide variety of empirically based techniques. Older techniques have been refined. New techniques, many of them stemming from modern learning theory, have emerged. Both old and new techniques are being quantified, assessed, and compared in group design research, and for the first time since modern therapy's beginnings in Freud, we are starting to ask, and answer, probing questions about the effectiveness of various treatment strategies.

PRIMARY PURPOSE OF THIS MANUAL

One such technique, which originated in the late 1930's, is *progressive relaxation training*. It is the primary purpose of this manual to set forth in detail the therapist behaviors necessary for effective application of this relaxation training technique. This book is *not* to be used for self-relaxation. Rather, the material presented here should provide therapists in many disciplines, including, for example, social work, pastoral counseling, and nursing, as well as psychology and psychiatry, with the skills they need to train their clients in relaxation.

To facilitate this goal, the book should be read *carefully* and *in its entirety.* Superficial familiarity with only a few of the basic procedures presented here, without an appreciation of the complexity of the technique, the limits of its applicability, and the problems which can arise in its use, is both ill-advised and irresponsible. Each chapter has been included because it is considered essential to the proper understanding of the relaxation technique, and each chapter should be thoroughly covered prior to any attempt at implementation.

HOW TO USE THE RECORD

The record accompanying this manual is intended to serve as a demonstration of the procedures described in Chapters 5 and 6; this record is *not* a substitute for the text. It is a *supplementary illustration* of the proper words, intonation, sequencing, and timing of the relaxation procedure. Perhaps the best way to use the record is to listen to it after reading Chapters 5 and 6. While the record is playing it may be helpful to refer to those chapters. (A complete session has *not* been recorded; only an *illustration* of correct procedures could be included.)

The record is *not* to be used with clients in training them in relaxation. A variety of recent experimental investigations have employed recorded relaxation instructions in training their subjects. As yet, however, there have been few adequate studies comparing the effects of recorded versus "live therapist" relaxation training. The research currently available suggests little success with recorded instructions (Paul and Trimble, 1970). The reader is therefore cautioned against using recorded instructions (even tapes designed for that purpose) until more definitive information is available.

USE OF THIS MANUAL IN RESEARCH

A second purpose of this manual involves its use in research. There are few manuals available which describe in detail the actual procedures used in relaxation training. As a result, most investigators develop their own abbreviated manuals in an attempt to standardize experimental procedures. But it sometimes happens that there is insufficiently detailed or improper statement of the procedures, so that the results of a particular experiment are meaningless. And when investigators use procedures that differ subtly from one another (in such factors as timing, rationale, and muscle groups), even if all these procedures result in "real" relaxation, results from one study are not comparable to the results of another. We hope that careful and widespread use of this manual in research will result in more valid and more comparable experimental investigations of these techniques.

As mentioned above, various researchers have used subtly differing procedures in training subjects in relaxation. Such differences have involved the amount of time per therapy hour spent in actual training, the total number of training sessions, the sequence of muscles used in tension-release cycles, the duration of tension and release, the number of tension-release cycles employed with each muscle group, and the use of suggestion in facilitating relaxation. The procedures outlined in Chapters 6 and 7 represent one possible combination of these variables. This particular combination was chosen on the basis of our experience with it, i.e. on its efficiency (in terms of amount of therapy time required for training) and effectiveness (in terms of success rate in a wide variety of clients). Unfortunately, little research is available to indicate precisely the optimum combination of variables, and attractive alternative possibilities are presented throughout the book. In general, it is suggested that standard procedures be followed, particularly in research use of the manual.

THE THERAPIST'S RESPONSIBILITY

Finally, while relaxation training procedures can be carefully specified, defined, sequenced, and, as a result, memorized, the therapist should not disregard other clinical skills and treat the client mechanically. The success of any technique is dependent upon the ability of the therapist to secure the client's confidence and cooperation. Consequently, building rapport and understanding with the client is an essential component of effective relaxation training. Progressive relaxation training, like most other therapy procedures, requires an adequate "delivery system" if its full potential for benefit is to be realized. We hope that progressive relaxation training will not be employed as a mechanical procedure taking place in an affectively neutral setting; rather it should be part of a joint effort by therapist and client, within the context of a positive therapeutic relationship, to develop in the client new skills for dealing with his/her problems.

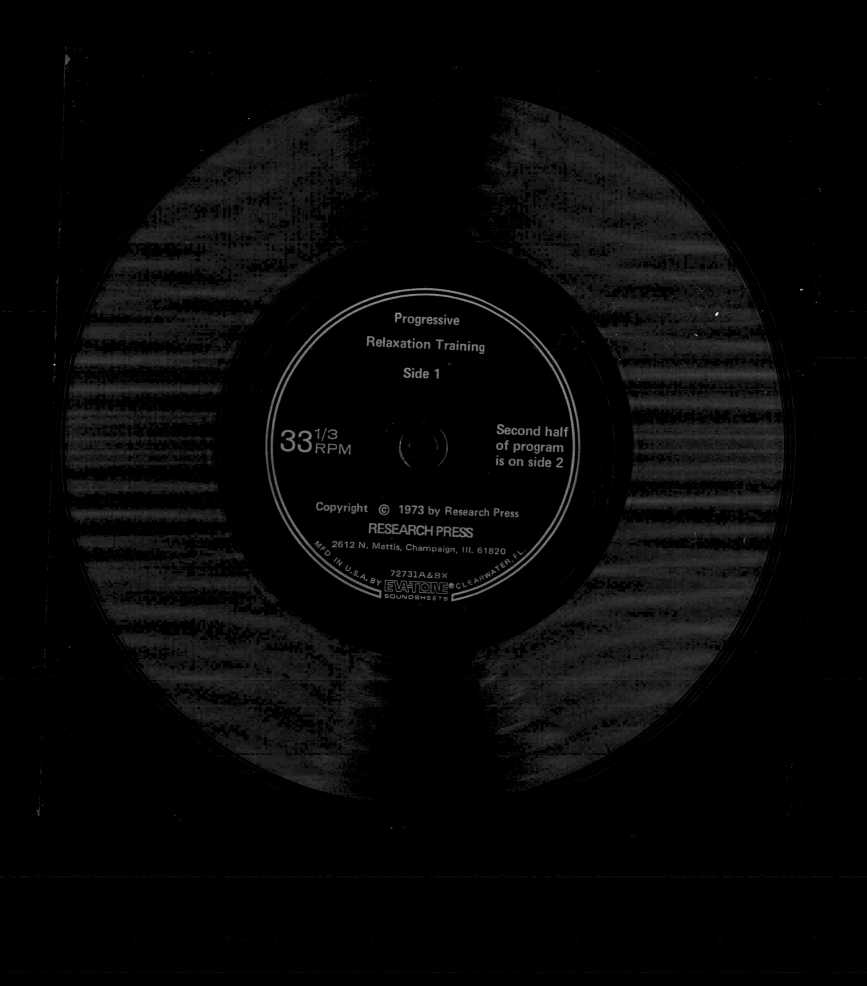

Progressive

Relaxation Training

Side 1

33 1/3 RPM

Second half
of program
is on side 2

Copyright © 1973 by Research Press

RESEARCH PRESS

2612 N. Mattis, Champaign, Ill. 61820

MFD IN U.S.A. BY   EVA·TONE® CLEARWATER, FL.

72731A&BX

SOUNDSHEETS

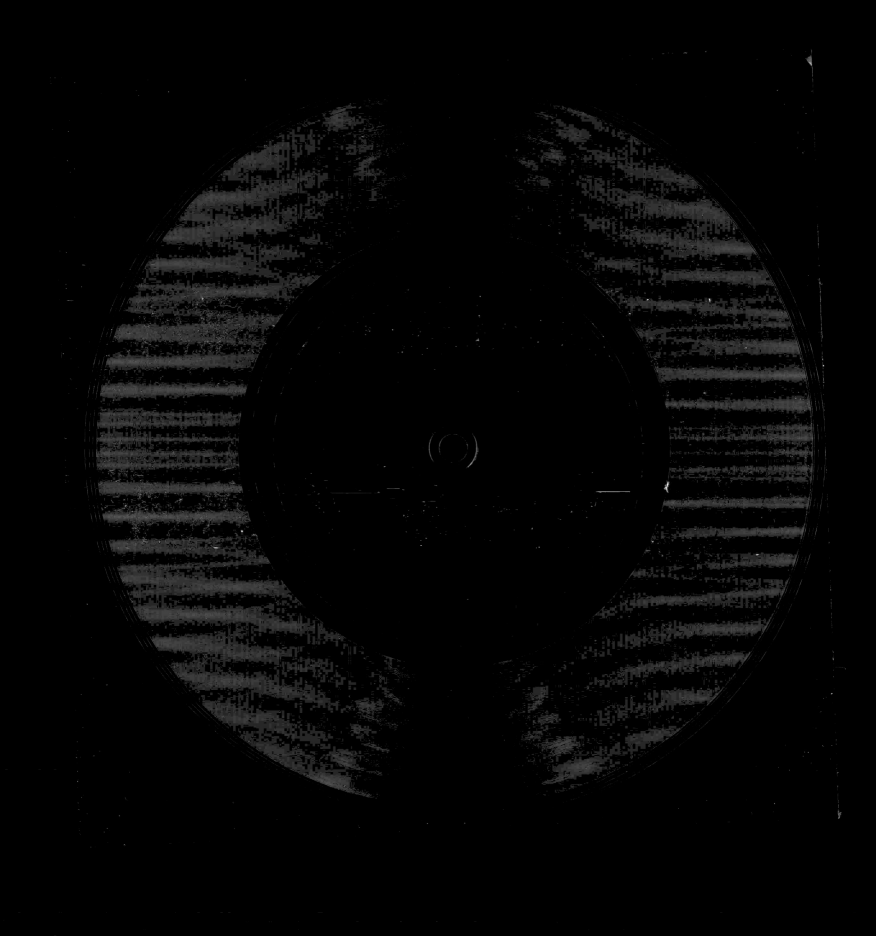

2 Background of Relaxation Training

HISTORY OF RELAXATION TRAINING

The history of relaxation training involves two distinct phases. The first phase began with the pioneering work of Edmund Jacobson who in 1934 developed a physiological method of combating tension and anxiety. The second phase was initiated by Joseph Wolpe, who modified Jacobson's procedures and applied them in a systematic program of treatment.

Edmund Jacobson

Jacobson began his work in 1908 at Harvard University. His early investigations led him to conclude that tension involved the effort manifested in the shortening of muscle fibers, that this tension occurred when a person reported "anxiety," and that such anxiety could be removed by eliminating the tension. Relaxation of muscle fibers, i.e. complete absence of all contractions, was seen as the direct physiological opposite of tension and was therefore a logical treatment for the overly tense or anxious person. He discovered that by systematically tensing and releasing various muscle groups and by learning to attend to and discriminate the resulting sensations of tension and relaxation a person may almost completely eliminate muscle contractions and experience a feeling of deep relaxation. The culmination of the studies was *Progressive Relaxation* (1938), a technical description of his theory and procedures. Four years earlier *You Must Relax* had been written as a layman's version of the same material. From 1936 to the 1960's Jacobson continued his investigations at the Laboratory for Clinical Physiology in Chicago. As of 1962 the basic relaxation procedure involved fifteen muscle groups. Each group was dealt with for from one to nine hour-long daily sessions before proceeding to the next group for a total of fifty-six sessions of systematic training.

Joseph Wolpe

The second phase in the development of this technique began with Joseph Wolpe's work in the counterconditioning of fear responses in 1948. His early studies with cats demonstrated that a conditioned fear reaction could be eliminated by evoking an incompatible response while gradually presenting the feared stimulus. The incompatible response will inhibit the fear response as long as the former is of greater intensity than the latter. In his search for an easily inducible incompatible response for humans, Wolpe discovered the techniques described in Jacobson's *Progressive Relaxation*. It seemed to him that relaxation, as a physiological opposite of tension, would be an ideal response for use in his counterconditioning program. However, the prohibitive amount of time required for Jacobsonian relaxation training resulted in two developments: (1) the use of, first, graduated real-life exposure and, later, graduated imagined exposure to the feared stimulus, and (2) modification of the relaxation training. The latter change resulted in a training program that could be completed in six 20-minute sessions with two 15-minute daily home practice sessions between training sessions. Wolpe's procedures were similar to Jacobson's in terms of tensing and releasing muscle groups in order to achieve deep relaxation. However, the therapist actually directed all aspects of the procedure through verbal instructions presented during the training sessions. Wolpe's therapists employed direct suggestion and even hypnotic procedures to facilitate awareness of bodily sensations.

The importance of Wolpe's work is twofold. First, the development of a more efficient relaxation program resulted in a great reduction in the amount of therapy time devoted to training. Secondly, treatment emphasis was placed on the circumstances surrounding the occurrence of anxiety rather than on the anxiety response itself. Certainly one could spend up to two hundred sessions in Jacobsonian training and achieve some clinical benefit. But anxiety is quite often a learned response to a certain stimulus, and it is most efficiently eliminated by developing an incompatible response (e.g. relaxation) *and* investigating the situations which elicit the anxiety. So rather than devoting a great deal of time to learning the adaptive response of relaxation, as in Jacobson's procedures, Wolpe shortened the process and used most of his therapy time to develop a structured situation-specific program of reconditioning of which relaxation was only one aspect. This particular treatment procedure, which has come to be known as *systematic desensitization*, is outlined in Wolpe's 1958 book *Psychotherapy by Reciprocal Inhibition*.

CURRENT STATUS OF PROGRESSIVE RELAXATION TRAINING

Since the time of Wolpe's first modification of Jacobson's training procedures, trends in the further development of relaxation training have been toward (1) specification of more efficient training conditions, (2) more refined measurement of the physiological effects of relaxation, and (3) determination of the behavioral problems most suited to treatment by relaxation training.

Unfortunately, the first trend has resulted in a flood of procedural variations which are unaccompanied by careful assessment of their differing effectiveness. Further, many of the training manuals produced are grossly lacking in both procedural detail and in clinical sensitivity. While no more could be expected from procedures designed for limited experimental programs, the danger exists that clinical application of these research manuals may occur.

Some definite empirical knowledge has resulted from the second trend. Decreased pulse rate and blood pressure have been shown by Jacobson to occur after relaxation training. A series of studies in the early 1960's demonstrated a lowering of skin conductance and respiration rate as a consequence of Wolpe's muscle relaxation procedures. More recently, in a carefully controlled study Paul found that a group of subjects given muscle

relaxation training exhibited greater decrease in subjective tension, heart rate, respiration rate, and muscle tension compared to a group who were simply told to relax themselves.

The questions posed by the third trend involve applications and extensions of the technique. Once a new therapy procedure is "discovered," implicit, or even explicit, claims that it can be used to treat any problem typically follow. Then as adequate research data are accumulated, enthusiasm wanes, and the hard task of evaluating the appropriateness of the technique and its place in a full-ranged treatment strategy begins. Relaxation training is currently in this phase.

At present there is enough case study evidence available to indicate the general range of target behaviors for which relaxation may be effectively employed, and these issues are discussed in Chapter 3. As for the use of progressive relaxation training within specific treatment strategies, much room for development remains. Already relaxation is used (1) in Wolpe's *systematic desensitization* technique, as a response incompatible with anxiety, (2) in *covert sensitization*,* as a means of increasing focused attention and image clarity, (3) in *differential relaxation*, as the principal basis of reducing tension throughout the day (see Chapter 8), and (4) in *anxiety relief* techniques as a supplementary pleasurable response conditioned to an anxiety-terminating cue word. Experimentation with relaxation as a component in other treatment programs continues, and it is hoped that future research will more clearly delineate its full range of application.

RESEARCH ON RELAXATION TRAINING

There are at least two reasons for the therapist to consider some of the experimental investigations of progressive relaxation procedures. First, it is important to document, for both colleagues and clients, the claims made for relaxation. Only with evidence supplied by

* Cautela, J. R. Covert Sensitization. Psychological Reports, 1967, Vol. 20, 459-468. Cautela, J. R. Treatment of Compulsive Behavior by Covert Sensitization. Psychological Record, 1966, Vol. 16, 33-41.

controlled research can we be confident in the effectiveness of the techniques we employ with our clients. Secondly, a careful look at studies involving relaxation may suggest areas for possible research and innovation and how to best approach those areas experimentally. The following presentation is by no means an exhaustive report of studies on progressive relaxation training; such a review is beyond the scope of this book. Rather, the four investigations presented below represent recent controlled research demonstrating the effects of progressive relaxation on physiological response systems and subjective experience.

Paul and his students have reported a series of investigations (1969a, 1969b, 1969c, 1970) concerning the effects of relaxation training. In the first of these studies (Paul, 1969a) the experimenter was examining the extent to which relaxation training reduced physiological arousal and subjective distress and resulted in effects different from those produced by either hypnotic suggestion or control procedures.

Comparative Effects of Relaxation Training

The sixty female college students who took part in the study were exposed to two half-hour experimental sessions identical in procedure and held seven days apart. One third of the subjects were trained in progressive relaxation, one third received direct hypnotic suggestion designed to produce relaxation, and the remaining control group was simply told to sit quietly and relax.

Dependent measures included pre- and post-assessment of self-reported anxiety (The Anxiety Differential; Husek and Alexander, 1963) and measures of physiological arousal (muscle tension, heart rate, skin conductance, and respiration rate) sampled during five periods in the sessions.

The results indicated significantly reduced discomfort and arousal within each session and, more importantly, significant differences among the three groups on all but the skin conductance measure. During the first session the progressive relaxation procedures resulted in greater relaxation by all measures than did control procedures. The progressive relaxation procedures also

produced greater heart rate and muscle tension decreases than did hypnotic induction; hypnosis produced greater reductions in respiration and subjective anxiety than control procedures did. During the second session the above results were replicated, except for additional reductions in heart rate and muscle tension in the hypnosis group compared to the control subjects. Paul concluded that, overall, progressive relaxation is superior to hypnotically induced or self-induced relaxation. The implications of this study are relevant to the discussions of hypnosis versus progressive relaxation in Chapter 11.

Possible Influence of Personality Characteristics

In his second report (1969b) Paul attempted to assess the relationship between successful relaxation performance and various personality characteristics of potential importance in predicting an individual's responsiveness to particular techniques. The Pittsburgh Social Extraversion—Introversion and Emotionality Scales (Bendig, 1962) were administered to the subjects of the previous study (Paul, 1969a) prior to the experimental procedures. These personality scores were later correlated with the subjective anxiety and physiological measures reported earlier. Additionally, prior to and immediately following each of the two experimental sessions the subjects were asked to visualize first a neutral scene and then an anxiety-provoking scene. The purpose of this was to assess the effects of relaxation, hypnosis, and control procedures on physiological responsiveness to stressful imagery.

Correlations of the personality scales with self-reported anxiety, physiology during training, and physiology during stressful imagery were, for the most part, not significant within each of the treatment conditions (relaxation, hypnosis, and control) and over all conditions. Paul concluded that responsiveness to relaxation or hypnotic procedures is not related to the personality dimensions of extraversion or emotionality.

There are, of course, other client characteristics which may be quite important in determining the success of relaxation training. Some of these, such as age and physical handicaps, are discussed in Chapter 3. But even in relatively homogeneous groups of clients the experienced relaxation trainer finds wide individual differences in depth of relaxation, rate of progress through the program, and the level of skill ultimately achieved. Doubtless many of these differences are a function of therapist behaviors, minor variations in procedure, and client motivation; but the possible influence of other factors within clients remains a potentially fruitful area of investigation. For example, we need to know more about how success at relaxation is related to the individual's ability to focus attention on internal sensations (and how to measure such ability). This behavior, as the reader will learn, is quite important in the development of the relaxation skill, and it seems reasonable to assume that differences in such an ability are likely to result in differences in the ultimate effect of training.

Relaxation and Stressful Imagery

Paul's third report (1969c) attempts to evaluate the use of progressive relaxation in decreasing physiological response to stressful imagery. Imagery data were collected on the same sixty subjects, and composite physiological responses to the stress scenes visualized before and after training were analysed. Arousal in response to the post-image increased for the self-relaxation control group and decreased for both hypnotically induced and progressive relaxation groups. The latter two groups demonstrated significantly lower physiological response than did the control group; and while the relaxation group evidenced the greatest *reduction* of response, the difference between relaxation and hypnosis group measures was not statistically significant. The author concluded that relaxation (progressive or hypnotic) does produce inhibition of physiological response to stressful visualizations.

Tape-Recorded Versus Live Presentation

The fourth and most recent study (Paul and Trimble, 1970) in this series investigated the efficacy of tape-recorded versus live (therapist present) relaxation train-ing. Thirty college females were assigned to one of three treatment conditions: progressive relaxation, hypnotically induced relaxation, and self-relaxation control. The procedures and measurements were identical to those employed in the previous studies, except that all training was conducted solely via tape-recorded instructions (therapist absent). The data from these tape-instructed groups were then compared to those from the previous studies conducted with live training.

Data analysis was limited to the second experimental session since it was at this stage that maximal differentiation of the treatment conditions had been found in the earlier studies. The data revealed that taped progressive relaxation was significantly inferior to live progressive relaxation. This finding was demonstrated in the heart rate, muscle tension, and response to stressful imagery measures. (The respiration rate difference approached significance.) Only on the subjective report measure was there any clear equivalence between taped and live presentation. No significant differences on any measure occurred between taped and live hypnosis or control conditions.

It is on the basis of these results and in light of the insufficiency of the data supporting tape-recorded relaxation that we strongly advise against the routine use of such procedures in either research or clinical settings (unless the particular tapes used can be shown to be equivalent in effectiveness to live presentations). In the research situation valid conclusions about the effects of relaxation are limited by Paul and Trimble's (1970) indication that no real relaxation is likely to take place. In a clinical situation not only is the client unlikely to achieve deep muscular relaxation, but the use of impersonal techniques such as taped instructions will do little to increase either the client's motivation or his/her confidence in the therapist.

FURTHER RESEARCH

On the basis of the evidence available from reasonably well-controlled research, we have some knowledge about (1) the general physiological and subjective effects of progressive relaxation training, (2) the specific effects of relaxation on the response to stressful imagery, and (3) the differences in the above effects produced by taped and live progressive relaxation, hypnotic suggestion, and self-relaxation. Unfortunately, beyond these previously discussed studies very little experimental research on progressive relaxation has been conducted. A series of investigations assessing the role of relaxation as a component of systematic desensitization (e.g. Rachman, 1965; Lomont and Edwards, 1967; Cooke, 1968; Folkins, Evans, Opton, and Lazarus, 1968; Johnson and Sechrest, 1968; Rachman, 1968; Zeisset, 1968; Laxer, Quarter, Kooman, and Walker, 1969; and Laxer and Walker, 1970)* has appeared, but research on the possible application of the relaxation technique alone to various target behaviors (see Chapter 3) is almost non-existent. Relevant studies are reviewed below, but it should be noted that the relaxation procedures used in all of them were more similar to hypnotic suggestion techniques than to progressive relaxation. They are included here because of the lack of research on progressive relaxation per se and because Paul's reports would suggest that progressive relaxation would probably have produced similar effects, differing only in magnitude.

Effect of Relaxation on Recall Abilities

Straughan and Dufort (1969) investigated the effects of verbally induced relaxation on the verbal learning and recall abilities in low- and high-anxiety subjects. Anxiety groups were chosen on the basis of Minnesota Multiphasic Personality Inventory scores. Subjects were assigned to one of four treatment conditions: (1) relaxation before the learning trial, (2) relaxation before the recall trial, (3) relaxation before both learning and recall trials, and (4) no relaxation at all. Half of each group was exposed to a learning trial of low difficulty paired associates, the other half to a high difficulty list.

---

* The general conclusion which can be drawn from these studies is that progressive muscle relaxation facilitates, but is not necessary for, the successful elimination of fear through desensitization.

Recall was tested immediately after exposure to the list and again forty-eight hours later. Using *latency* (time interval between question and reply) as the dependent measure, the investigators found that the effects of relaxation differed as a function of the anxiety level. On the immediate recall test, relaxation produced faster responding in the high-anxious subjects and slower responding in low-anxious subjects when compared to non-relaxed subjects with the same anxiety levels. Relaxation effects were greater for high difficulty lists than for low difficulty lists. On the delayed recall test, relaxed high-anxious subjects again responded faster and relaxed low-anxious subjects slower than their non-relaxed counterparts. Additionally, relaxation before the learning trial intensified this effect as compared to relaxation before recall.

There are two important implications in these results. First, the therapist must be sure he/she is dealing with an anxious client before embarking on a relaxation program (see Chapter 3). Secondly, any verbal learning that takes place during traditional verbal therapy is likely to be influenced both by the anxiety level of the client and by the extent to which the therapist provides a comfortable atmosphere by using relaxation or in some other way. (This suggests an important area of research directly related to relaxation procedures.)

Aiding Psychotic Children

A rare attempt to apply relaxation-like procedures to psychotic children has been reported by Graziano and Kean (1968). They found that operant reinforcement of social behavior in four autistic children had decreased the intensity and duration of tantrums but had had little effect on frequency. High excitement and tension in response to minor irritations seemed to occur prior to these outbursts. Consequently, brief, highly structured relaxation training was initiated. This procedure simply involved having the children lie down while the investigators gently massaged their arms, legs, and neck, at the same time instructing them to breathe easily and relax. Rewards were given for relaxed behavior during these sessions. The investigators reported that over the one hundred and five brief sessions the children learned to become quiet and relaxed during the sessions and that outbursts outside the sessions decreased to zero.

This study did not determine whether these sessions were effective because of the increased opportunity to reward desirable behavior or because of the relaxation training itself. However, a hyperactive adolescent has been treated using standard relaxation procedures alone. This child was also in an operantly-oriented behavior modification program, but several months of rewarding non-hyperactive behavior had failed to modify the child's rapid staggered speech and jerky body movements. The relaxation training itself, without specific rewards for looking relaxed or reporting relaxation, resulted in reports from other staff members of decreases in the problem behaviors. Obviously, controlled group research on the effects of relaxation on hyperactive and/or aggressive children is needed.

Case Studies Involving Insomnia

Kahn, Baker, and Weiss (1968) have reported the use of *autogenic* (self-hypnotically induced) relaxation to treat college students reporting chronic insomnia. Two half-hour group training sessions were given each week for two weeks. Post-training interviews indicated that eleven of thirteen subjects had improved. Among ten subjects who, prior to training, had estimated the amount of time before falling asleep, all reported shorter times after training. At a ten-week follow-up, seven subjects reported less difficulty than prior to training, one had relapsed, and five were consistently falling asleep within ten minutes. Finally, at an eleven-month follow-up interview, eleven of twelve contacted subjects reported sleeping better than before treatment. These results, however, are open to a variety of explanations other than the effectiveness of the relaxation therapy per se: placebo and expectancy effects, repeated observation, extra-therapy experiences, maturational processes, statistical regression, etc. (Campbell and Stanley, 1963). The study has also been criticized (1) for confounding relaxation therapy with Rogerian interviewing and demand characteristics and (2) for using self-report as the only outcome measure (Eisenman, 1970).

Geer and Katkin (1966) have reported the successful treatment of a case of severe insomnia via relaxation and systematic desensitization. After several relaxation training sessions the client was exposed to single-item desensitization: the client repeatedly visualized herself attempting to fall asleep while she was in a state of deep relaxation. As the investigators themselves pointed out, however, there is no way to conclude whether desensitization contributed any beneficial effects over and beyond the relaxation training.

Clearly, the available references on the psychological treatment of insomnia are limited and involve uncontrolled designs. While some promise of effective modification via relaxation or variants of relaxation is offered by such case studies, controlled investigations are required.

Controlled Research on Insomnia

In September 1971 the second author began pilot projects to assess the feasibility of large scale insomnia research on a college population. At that time group testing of 650 University of Iowa students in Introductory Psychology revealed that 18% of that population felt both that they had a sleeping problem and that they would be willing to volunteer for a study of treatment techniques aimed at eliminating sleep disturbance. A more specific frequency breakdown of reported average *sleep-onset latency* (time between entering sleep situation and the reported onset of sleep) was obtained in the fall of 1972:

No. of minutes to sleep onset	No. of students	% of students
1-5	53	10.2
6-10	133	25.6
11-15	122	23.5
16-20	68	13.1
21-25	23	4.4
26-30	40	7.7
31-45	58	11.1

No. of minutes to sleep onset	No. of students	% of students
46-60	14	2.7
61-90	4	.8
91-120	3	.6
120 +	1	.2

Since Paul (1969a) had demonstrated differential reduction of physiological arousal among progressive, hypnotic, and self-relaxation control procedures, the initial outcome study assessed the effectiveness of these three techniques in eliminating moderate insomnia (Borkovec and Fowles, 1973). Female college students who reported sleeping difficulty were selected on the basis of the following criteria: (1) report of average latency of sleep onset of more than 30 minutes, (2) no current use of drugs, and (3) current uninvolvement with other professional services. Forty subjects were given a packet of daily sleep questionnaires with instructions to fill out a questionnaire upon awakening each morning until one week after the last therapy session. Within blocks of initial severity, as determined in the assessment interview, subjects were randomly assigned to one of the three relaxation conditions (all modeled after Paul, 1969a) or to waiting-list no-treatment. Four male graduate students served as therapists, each therapist administering individual treatment to subjects from each condition. Each subject received three one-hour therapy sessions plus instructions to practice the relaxation techniques just before going to bed. All three treated groups reported significant improvement after therapy while the no-treatment group showed no change. Progressive and hypnotic relaxation both produced significantly greater improvement than did no-treatment. Self-relaxation effects did not differ markedly from the other relaxation techniques.

This first controlled study of insomnia gave supporting evidence of the effectiveness of relaxation techniques in general, but the nearly equal improvement of the self-relaxation control procedure raised interpre-

tive problems. The subjects may have been responding on the self-report measures solely to the demand characteristics of the experiment and sleep disturbance was not substantially modified, or sleep disturbance may have lessened in all three treated groups but as a function of suggestion, therapist contact, expectancy, and other factors.

The second study (Steinmark and Borkovec, 1973) represented an attempt to eliminate the demand problem and to establish procedures whereby self-report data may be validly used in outcome research. Critical to the control procedures in this experiment was the use of counter-demand instructions: all treated subjects were told not to expect improvement in sleep disturbance until after the last (fourth) therapy session. Forty-eight sleep-disturbed college students were randomly assigned to one of four conditions: progressive relaxation, relaxation plus desensitization of the sleep situation, placebo, and waiting-list no-treatment. Placebo involved the presentation of chronologically ordered bedtime behaviors in a quasi-desensitization procedure; relaxation training, however, was not administered to this group. Two male graduate student therapists each treated one half of the subjects in each condition. Four therapy sessions were given to groups of five to seven subjects. Relaxation and desensitization groups reported significantly greater improvement in latency of sleep onset than did the placebo and no-treatment groups, even during the counter-demand period. Relaxation and desensitization groups did not differ from each other. After the fourth therapy session all three treated groups reported significantly greater improvement than did no-treatment. These results support the effectiveness of progressive relaxation therapy (common to both relaxation and desensitization) in the treatment of moderate insomnia. Most importantly, this conclusion is strengthened by the use of a strategic demand manipulation. Despite demand instructions incompatible with reports of improvement both relaxation and desensitization groups indicated reduction in sleep disturbance while placebo reported no change.

3 Targets for Relaxation Training

Relaxation training is not a panacea and should not be presented as such to clients. It is a technique which does have considerable value for the alleviation of a limited range of difficulties in a limited range of individuals. In order to avoid wasting time and effort, therapists should be aware of the kinds of problems and situations for which relaxation training seems most appropriate. The following material is not meant to be an exhaustive list of all possible client and situation targets (therapist ingenuity will constantly be providing new applications of "limited" techniques); rather, this is an outline of those situations in which relaxation training has been beneficial and those situations in which it has proved less useful.

WHO CAN BENEFIT FROM RELAXATION TRAINING

It should be noted that, while relaxation training procedures can elevate the therapist's status ("placebo value") in the eyes of the client, the therapist should not teach all clients these skills simply to impress them. Since relaxation training is primarily for clients with high tension levels, where tension is not of major concern the use of relaxation training can result in an unimpressed, if not hostile, client who experiences no noticeable change in an already low level of tension. Thus, while tense clients are often very grateful for having been taught relaxation skills, individuals whose problems do not involve significant tension will react quite differently.

The most obviously appropriate targets for relaxation training are uncomfortably high-level tension responses which interfere with the performance of other behavior. These responses may include insomnia (caused by muscular tension and intrusive thoughts), tension headaches (which have not responded to prescribed medication), and less specific complaints of "general tenseness" or "tight nerves" which seem to be more related to just being awake than to any particular stimulus situation.* (Some specific examples of these kinds of cases appear later in this chapter.)

Of course, while individuals whose tension levels do not cause them any difficulties will probably profit little from learning relaxation skills *in a therapy setting*, they would not be disadvantaged for having acquired such skills (preferably in a non-therapy context). On the contrary, it is easy to imagine that almost anyone who ever experiences tension would be glad to have a pleasant and efficient means of eliminating it, either in actual tension situations or just at the end of a long day. It has been our experience, in fact, that the "normal" volunteer subjects in our practice training programs almost always report that their new skill is extremely useful to them on an everyday basis. Obviously we do not feel that anyone could be considered "worse off" following progressive relaxation training (provided that it was conducted in an appropriate manner), but in this book we will be focusing on the *clinical* uses of the training.

PRE-TRAINING INVENTORY

In clinical situations the unwise use of progressive relaxation training can have negative effects, mainly on the client's motivation and cooperativeness. Therefore, the techniques should not be employed without careful consideration, even in cases where there is clear discomfort or disruption. There are three general areas the clinician should explore before deciding to include progressive relaxation training in the total therapeutic program.

---

* While this type of problem is usually referred to as "free-floating anxiety," it can often be related more specifically to environmental events. However, the limited therapeutic contact for which this manual is designed will not allow detailed functional analysis of the situation.

Medical Clearance

The first involves medical clearance. In cases where relaxation training is being considered as a means of eliminating a physical complaint, such as headaches or low back pain, the therapist should make certain that (1) there is no strictly organic basis for the complaint which could be more directly treated with drugs, (2) there are no indications counter to the use of relaxation training (such as the inadvisability of having the client tense certain muscle groups), (3) relaxation of relevant muscle groups is desirable (in some cases of low back pain, for example, strengthening of certain muscles is preferred over learning to relax them), and (4) it is possible to have the client discontinue the use of drugs, such as strong tranquilizers, which are designed to produce muscle relaxation. (Skill at relaxation is more easily acquired and more beneficial when learned in the absence of such drugs; see Chapter 11.) The therapist should consult with the client's physician on these points.

Discovering the Causes of the Reported Tension

The second area of inquiry concerns the possible reactivity of reported tension. That is, does the client feel overly tense in situations where tension of disruptive intensity is inappropriate, or is the discomfort a rational response to realistic circumstances? Let us take the case of an insomniac. If this person's difficulty in getting to sleep is primarily the result of (1) being "tight" in a situation calling for relaxation and/or (2) difficulty in refocusing attention away from daily problems, then relaxation training may be entirely appropriate. If, on the other hand, the person is on the verge of financial disaster or regularly receives threatening phone calls, then relaxation training alone, without additional actions resolving these realistic crises, is likely to be of only transient aid.

Clearly, before initiating a program of relaxation training, the therapist must decide if it is realistic to expect an increase in relaxation skill to be a significant factor in alleviating the client's problems. If it seems that the disruptive tension comes in response to a serious and definable problem in living, then it is probably better to deal with that external problem than with the tension it creates. If, however, it is clear that the client is over-responding to all of life's major *and* minor problems, then relaxation may be quite helpful.

Finding Possible Stimuli for the Tension Response

These considerations lead into the third issue to be faced prior to deciding upon relaxation training as part of a therapy strategy. If the therapist considers the client's tension problem to be the result of anxiety which has been conditioned to specific environmental stimuli, relaxation therapy alone should not be expected to alleviate the problem. In such cases relaxation training is often employed as part of a more extensive therapeutic program such as systematic desensitization. The degree to which a client's problem is conditioned to a specific environmental stimulus can be determined through clinical interviews.

Returning for a moment to our hypothetical case of insomnia, the client may find it difficult to sleep because of anxiety associated with specific aspects of the sleeping situation, such as darkness, nocturnal noises, or fear of burglars. If this is the case, the probability that relaxation training alone could permanently inhibit tension in the feared situation would be low. In fact, there is considerable evidence that relaxation alone would be ineffective in this situation (Cooke, 1968; Davidson, 1968; Lang and Lazovik, 1963; Lang, Lazovik, and Reynolds, 1965). There is always the chance that the original estimate of the problem was incorrect and that relaxation training alone *can* handle the problem in question. This would become clear quite early in systematic desensitization treatment; we have often found that by the time the program of training in progressive relaxation in preparation for desensitization is completed, relaxation training alone has resulted in rather dramatic improvements in the situation. More often, of course, no such improvement occurs, and the original hypothesis (i.e. that the tension is the result of a specifically conditioned anxiety response which is too strong to be inhibited for a very long period of time by relaxation alone) is confirmed, and systematic desensitization is carried out to completion.

The therapist should not expect progressive relaxation training to be effective in every situation involving disruptive tension. Many factors concerning the reported tension will determine whether progressive relaxation is to be used alone as a first step in treatment or as part of a more extensive therapeutic program. We hope that the case material presented at the end of this chapter will help to illustrate this decision-making process.

THE CLIENT

We have been considering the range of problems for which relaxation training seems appropriate. Let us now turn our attention to the client. Success at learning relaxation skills requires only that the client (1) be able to give continued focused attention to the muscles of his/her body (and to the voice of the therapist), (2) be able to systematically tense and release specified muscle groups, and (3) regularly practice the skills learned in training sessions. These requirements would eliminate most very young children (for whom relaxation training alone would probably be inappropriate anyway) from the target population.

In addition, individuals with major physical handicaps such as partial paralysis would be difficult students in relaxation training, though the therapist's ingenuity in devising alternative tensing strategies (see Chapter 5) may surmount such obstacles. Muscle groups which are no longer under voluntary control might be bypassed with little or no loss of benefit to the client. If the problem in a handicapped client seems an appropriate target for relaxation training, the therapist should at least attempt such training, with those modifications dictated by the client's physical condition, rather than abandon the idea *a priori*. Of course, if the client's disability would prevent the muscle groups from tensing on cue, the value of even a preliminary effort at training would be questionable. The therapist must make a judgment,

weighing possible benefits of successful training against the effects of a failure experience.

There is no upper limit on the age of clients who might benefit from relaxation training as long as the requirements stated above are met.

CASE EXAMPLES

In this section we shall present some case materials to illustrate more specifically the types of problems and clients suitable for progressive relaxation training. The cases described are from case work done by the authors or their colleagues and are offered as examples of situations in which progressive relaxation training is appropriate.

Reducing Tension for Therapy Communication

One of the most basic and important ways in which progressive relaxation training can be employed is by using it to reduce a client's inability to discuss emotionally-charged interview topics. Relaxation training very early in therapy can facilitate discussion of such issues through (1) direct reduction of tension in the interview situation and (2) development of a positive client-therapist relationship. Often after a tense client has participated in one or two relaxation training sessions and experienced lower arousal, at least in the session itself, he/she is more likely to "open up" since the therapist has already demonstrated an ability to intervene in a positive fashion. Whether or not relaxation training is an integral part of the client's therapy program, it may have served a valuable catalytic role.

As an example of this, a woman in her late thirties was referred by her social worker to one of the authors after complaining of severe nervousness and general emotional upset. In the initial interview the therapist noted that the client's tension level was so high that she was unable to remain focused on the conversation. She responded in irrelevant ways to direct questions, made repeated vague references to persons who were "against" her, moved randomly from topic to topic, and in general could not describe the problems for which she sought help.

Instead of continuing the assessment interview, the therapist told the client that, because she seemed so upset, she would probably benefit by learning to bring at least some of her tension under control. Fortunately, she was able to concentrate on what he said and she seemed enthusiastic about the idea of relaxation, though skeptical about its ability to work for her. Although she probably could not fully concentrate on all details of the abbreviated rationale for the procedure (see Chapter 5), she was very cooperative and followed instructions with only minor errors.

Following the first relaxation session, the client expressed astonishment at really having felt relaxed. She stated that she could not remember a time prior to that session when she did not feel extremely "tight" and she found the contrast "amazing." At this point, the pace of her speech had slowed considerably and she sounded more "normal."

At the second session the relaxation training was repeated with similar results. By the second session the therapist could begin to explore the client's reasons for seeking help, and this time she was able to clearly describe some problems relating to family, ideas of persecution by neighbors, and somatic discomfort. These were then dealt with, first by the therapist in one additional session and then by the client's social worker.

Aiding Clients with Tension-Caused Illnesses

Progressive relaxation training can also be employed in many cases where tension has resulted in actual tissue damage and consequent physical illness. This is well illustrated by the case of a professional man in his fifties who came to one of the authors because of "chronic tension" which had resulted in a serious stomach ulcer. He described himself (and his report was corroborated informally by those who knew him) as being difficult to get along with, "high-strung," and in a great deal of physical pain most of the time as a result of the ulcer. He was taking tranquilizers several times a day in addition to his ulcer medication.

The therapist told him that while relaxation training could not cure his ulcer directly it might alleviate much of the tension which aggravated it, thus allowing some healing to take place. The client agreed to participate in the training and to discontinue use of his tranquilizers (this step was taken in consultation with the client's physician and was designed to maximize the benefits of relaxation training; see Chapter 11).

The client was extremely cooperative during training and practiced faithfully between sessions. After five weekly meetings he was able to reliably produce deep relaxation on his own by the recall procedure (see Chapter 7) and training was terminated (this particular training program was completed unusually quickly due to time pressure; normally the more extended schedule presented in Chapter 7 is followed).

The client was extremely pleased with the results of the program. To the therapist's knowledge he never again had to resort to tranquilizers. He was generally more relaxed and better able to deal with the tension-producing aspects of his job through use of his relaxation skill at the office and at the end of the day. There was also an overall reduction in stomach pain. An unexpected side benefit was also noted when another therapist who was working on other problems with the client and his family in a group situation spontaneously reported a decrease in the client's level of tension and irritability and a simultaneous increase in responsiveness in the group meetings. It is reasonable to hypothesize that these changes, while not brought about directly by relaxation training, were greatly facilitated by it.

Eliminating Insomnia

As suggested by experimental research reported in Chapter 2, progressive relaxation training, either alone or in combination with other procedures, is often very helpful in cases of tension-produced insomnia. In some instances the client's problem results from a high level of residual tension, and other clients are troubled by bothersome thoughts at bedtime. Still others are kept awake by tension associated with external noises or other stimuli.

The use of relaxation training alone in dealing with the residual tension/intrusive thoughts insomnia is well illustrated by the case of a female graduate student in her mid-twenties. She reported being unable to relax at bedtime because of residual muscle tension stemming from the day's activity and because she could not stop her mind from "racing" with thoughts of recent events and future plans. Careful assessment of her situation showed that these thoughts were not based on any realistic problem in her life, and relaxation training was begun. The client learned the procedures quickly and arranged to practice them at home in the afternoon and immediately before bed.

The therapist suggested that the bedtime practice session take place while the client was actually in bed and ready to go to sleep. The program resulted in an almost immediate reduction in the client's sleeping problem. In fact, she reported that she was falling asleep during the bedtime practice session before completing the practice. In addition, she found that once she had fallen asleep she was awakened less often by noises in neighboring apartments. When she was awakened by her roommate or by some unusually loud noise in the building, she found it much easier to get to sleep again through the abbreviated use of relaxation.

The client reported that the program helped her to lose muscular tightness, especially after a very busy day, and to focus her attention away from thoughts that would keep her awake.

A more complex type of insomnia problem was presented by a woman in her early thirties. She was troubled by a wide variety of specific fears, several persistent and severe somatic complaints (all of which had been shown to have no organic base), depression, and general anxiety. In the process of assessing this client's many complaints, it was discovered that a major aggravating factor was fatigue caused by a pattern of intermittent sleep. The client reported that she was easily awakened by the slightest sound and that, upon awakening, would think about the possibility that someone was attempting to break into the house to kill her. Her husband had attempted to reduce the problem by installing more than adequate locks on all the doors and windows, but the sleeping pattern remained unchanged.

One of the first of many procedures employed with this client was progressive relaxation training. It was felt that an overall reduction in day-to-day tension through practice sessions and *differential relaxation* (see Chapter 8) would pave the way for intervention in the other target areas. In addition, it was hoped that the client could use the relaxation skill at night to get to sleep and to return to sleep if she awoke during the night.

In order to decrease the probability that fear of burglars would interfere with the use of relaxation skills, the client was asked to check before going to bed that all doors and windows were locked. If she was awakened during the night by a sound and began to worry about an intruder, she was told to get up immediately and check all doors and windows again, then use relaxation to get back to sleep.

The client learned relaxation easily and there was an immediate reduction in difficulty in getting to sleep. In addition, after only one instance of re-checking door and window locks (followed by the use of relaxation to fall asleep), the client began to sleep soundly and continuously every night. These self-reports were corroborated by independent interviews with the client's husband.

Differential relaxation was later used to reduce her tension when she took a driver's test, to help her overcome her fear of flying, and in other tension-producing situations.

A final case involving sleeping problems well illustrates the way in which progressive relaxation can be used, in combination with other procedures, to deal with very strong learned anxiety. The case really involved *in vivo* (in real-life situation) *desensitization* but is included here to show how relaxation procedures can be modified to meet specific situational needs.*

The client was a female college student who had long-standing fears of fire, of the dark, and of being alone. She insisted that the lights be left on in her room

* The authors wish to thank Dr. Lester Tobias for making this case report available.

all night and that another person be in the room while she slept. These requirements had always been met in the past. But the client was to leave for study abroad seven weeks after her first contact with the therapist, and she was anticipating that these accommodations would not be made and that she would not be able to complete her stay.

The client also experienced vivid images of burning people and great fires when attempting to go to sleep in the dark. Keeping the room lit and another person with her eased the "panic," but there was always great difficulty in falling asleep. Three years before her contact with the therapist, the client's aunt had been killed in a night fire. This incident had aggravated the problem considerably.

The time limit imposed by the client's departure made the use of a full program of relaxation and systematic desensitization impractical. Instead, a variant of progressive relaxation combined with self-administered *in vivo desensitization* was employed. Progressive relaxation training was begun toward the end of the second interview. To save time, the rationale was abbreviated and each of the sixteen muscle groups was tensed and relaxed only once. The client was instructed to practice more fully at home, and one of the two daily practice sessions was to occur at bedtime. The client did very well at relaxing even in the first session and practiced regularly.

In addition to using relaxation at bedtime, the client was to gradually reduce the amount of illumination in the room each night and relax for sleep at a time which was progressively earlier than the time her roommate arrived and retired. This program was designed to gradually expose the client to more and more difficult stimulus situations in the presence of deep relaxation.

At the third interview the client reported that her fears had greatly decreased and that they seemed less overwhelming because of her growing ability to use relaxation to get to sleep. The relaxation training sessions and *in vivo* practice procedures continued for three more weeks, at which time the client reported no fearful visualizations and no problems in falling asleep. At the last session the client reported that she had recently been at a friend's house when it caught fire and that her behavior had been rational and appropriate. She experienced no maladaptive anxiety following the incident.

4 The Physical Setting

As mentioned before, thorough knowledge of and experience with the relaxation procedures, as well as the use of other general clinical skills, are all essential aspects of effective relaxation training. A third component involves the physical environment in which training takes place. The effectiveness of the training will increase as more care is taken to provide a suitable setting for the training.

If the therapist remembers this general rule, there should be little difficulty in insuring a proper physical setting: do everything possible to increase the client's ability to focus attention on sensations of tension and relaxation. In other words, eliminate all sources of extraneous stimulation.

THE CONSULTING ROOM

Relaxation training should take place in a quiet, attractive room. Most therapists' offices meet this requirement anyway, but frequently training has to be done elsewhere, and other environments must be carefully prepared. While a soundproof room would be ideal, almost any room may be used. Windows and doors should be closed and drapes drawn to eliminate sights and sounds from the outside. Ringing telephones, pounding typewriters, and talking people disrupt relaxation, and it would be wise to take all possible steps to reduce this disruption to a minimum. Bell volume can be easily decreased on most standard telephones. Secretaries may be requested to postpone their typing. A sign on the door reading, "Quiet, please," will help avoid conversations in front of the door. Humming air-conditioners or ventilation systems are no problem as long as they are not loud since clients readily adapt to continuous sound.

Proper lighting in the room is also important. Ideally, one would prefer a completely dark room to facilitate concentration; however, for two reasons this is impractical. First, the therapist needs some light in order to time various phases of training and to watch the client for signs of proper or improper relaxing. Second, an anxious client might become more anxious by being in a dark room with a relative stranger. The client should be told in the initial instructions that the room lights will be be dimmed and why this is necessary (see Chapter 5). The consulting room should contain a flexible desk lamp which has a shade that can be adjusted so the client does not receive any direct lighting. It is wise to turn this light on before turning off other lights in the room in order to avoid stumbling around a dark room in search of the desk lamp.

THE CHAIR

An important consideration is the chair the client uses during relaxation training. The following guideline will help the therapist in making arrangements for a chair: the client should be *completely supported* by the chair (there should be no need for any exertion to maintain body support). There are two reasons for this: (1) having to use any muscles for support would interfere with concentration on the process of relaxing other muscles, and (2) any muscles required for support would not be able to relax.

The ideal chair is a well-padded recliner chair. In such a chair the client can sit back with legs and arms extended and supported by comfortably padded arm and leg rests. A pillow may be used to eliminate head-turns and consequent use of neck muscles.

Of course, any overstuffed chair or wide couch may be used as an alternative as long as the basic requirement of complete support is met. Small pillows may help a client who is having difficulty finding a comfortable position. Because people differ in size and shape, the therapist may have to use some ingenuity in making the client completely comfortable on the available furniture.

The therapist should watch for reports of numbness (the "falling asleep") of various parts of the body, particularly the arms and legs. This is usually the result of poor circulation caused by pressure on the blood vessels. A slight change in position of the limbs should eliminate this problem.

THE CLIENT'S DRESS

The final aspect of the physical environment is the client's clothing and accessories. Since there is usually at least one assessment interview prior to the initiation of relaxation training, the therapist should suggest to the client that he/she wear comfortable, loose-fitting clothing at the next session. The client should wear slacks and a comfortable shirt or blouse (with loose-fitting undergarments). Comfortable skirts and dresses are acceptable, though wearing them may cause some embarrassment due to the necessity of a prone position during relaxation. Contact lens wearers should be asked to wear regular glasses, if possible, to eliminate time-consuming removal of the lenses. At the session the therapist should suggest removal of glasses, watches, and shoes to reduce extraneous stimulation and to allow for free movement.

If practicality and good taste allow, the above suggestions should be followed. If any aspect of the physical recommendation is not feasible, it should be as closely approximated as is possible. The important consideration is that maximum physical and psychological comfort for the client is achieved.

5 Session I: The Rationale

The first session of relaxation training is perhaps the most important simply because it is at this point that the therapist should, through proper explanation and justification of the procedures to follow, instill in the client feelings of confidence in both the therapist and the technique, as well as enthusiasm for carrying out the "homework." In addition, the therapist's initial execution of the actual relaxation procedures should be such that the client experiences significant and pleasant reduction of tension. Thus, at the conclusion of a successful first session the client should thoroughly appreciate both the procedures and the need for his/her cooperation, including regular practice. The client should have a "feel" for what deep relaxation is and the expectation that, even though the first attempt was good, future sessions will show continued improvement.

PRESENTING THE RATIONALE

The following material is an illustration of a first session of relaxation training. It is *not* a script to be memorized and repeated in the presence of a client. Any attempt to copy the style of the recorded example will probably not be satisfactory since the words and sentence structures used will not suit most therapists and will sound stilted, unnatural, and inconsistent with other verbal behavior of the therapist. The therapist should at all times maintain an air of warmth, confidence, and competence; struggling to reproduce a prepared speech will not help communicate those qualities to the client.

The therapist should include the content outlined below, as well as attempt to provide the atmosphere illustrated on the record, but the specific words and phrases should be those with which the therapist is comfortable. In other words, the therapist should learn the *content* of the first session and communicate this content in his/her own words.

Another reason for avoiding a set speech in the first session is that, because clients differ in intelligence and sophistication, the level of explanation and choice of words must be adjusted to suit the client's particular needs. The therapist should remain flexible enough to successfully communicate to any client.

The first *relaxation* session should begin with an effort to place the client's tension in the proper perspective. If the only complaint is sleeplessness and relaxation training seems appropriate (see Chapter 3), the tension involved would be given a central position in the conceptualization of the client's difficulties. If, on the other hand, the tension to be dealt with is only one of the target behaviors or if relaxation training is being used mainly to allow the client to discuss other problems calmly, the therapist should make it clear that this is the case. Thus, the therapist should explain to the client the role of tension in the total problem situation and to what extent reduction of that tension can be expected to result in improvement. The therapist should make sure that the client (1) accepts this estimation of the case and (2) feels that application of the relaxation procedure seems valid. Some clients may be somewhat skeptical of this second point, but they should at least be willing to give full cooperation and withhold final judgment.

Once the client recognizes tension as at least a part of the problem, the therapist can begin the more formal portion of rationale presentation. An illustration of the standard rationale follows.

AN ILLUSTRATION
OF THE STANDARD RATIONALE

The procedures I have been discussing in terms of reducing your tension are collectively called progressive relaxation training. They were first developed in the 1930's by a physiologist named Jacobson, and in recent years we have modified his original technique in order to make it simpler and more effective. Basically, progressive relaxation training consists of learning to sequentially tense and then relax various groups of muscles all through the body, while at the same time paying very close and careful attention to the feelings associated with both tension and relaxation. That is, in addition to teaching you how to relax, I will also be encouraging you to learn to recognize and pinpoint tension and relaxation as they appear in everyday situations as well as in our sessions here.

You should understand quite clearly that learning relaxation skills is very much like learning any other kind of skill such as swimming, or golfing, or riding a bicycle; thus in order for you to get better at relaxing you will have to practice doing it just as you would have to practice other skills. It is very important that you realize that progressive relaxation training involves learning on your part; there is nothing magical about the procedures. I will not be doing anything *to* you; I will merely be introducing you to the technique and directing your attention to various aspects of it, such as the presence of certain feelings in the muscles. Thus, without your active cooperation and regular practicing of the things you will learn today, the procedures are of little use.

Now I mentioned earlier that I will be asking you to tense and then relax various groups of muscles in your body. You may be wondering why, if we want to produce relaxation, we start off by producing tension. The reason is that, first of all, everyone is always at some level of tension during his waking hours; if a person were not tense to *some* extent, he would simply fall down. The amount of tension actually present in everyday life differs, of course, from individual to individual and we say that each person has reached some adaptation level—the amount of tension under which he operates day to day.

The goal of progressive relaxation training is to help you learn to reduce muscle tension in your body far below your adaptation level at any time you wish to do so. In order to accomplish this, I could ask you to focus your attention, for example, on the muscles in your right hand and lower arm and to then just let them relax. Now you might think you can let these muscles drop down below their adaptation level just by "letting them go" or whatever, and to a certain extent, you probably can. However, in progressive relaxation, we want you to learn to produce larger and very much more noticeable reductions in tension and the best way to do this is first to produce a good deal of tension in the muscle group (i.e. raise the tension well above adaptation level) and then, all at once, release that tension. The release creates a "momentum" which allows the muscles to drop well below adaptation level. The effect is like that which we could produce with a pendulum which is hanging motionless in a vertical position. If we want it to swing far to the right, we could push it quite hard in that direction. It would be much easier, however, to start by pulling the pendulum in the opposite direction and then letting it go. It will swing well past the vertical point and continue in the direction we want it to go.

Thus, tensing muscle groups prior to letting them relax is like giving ourselves a "running start" toward deep relaxation through the momentum created by the tension release. Another important advantage to creating and releasing tension is that it will give you a good chance to focus your attention upon and become clearly aware of what tension really feels like in each of the various groups of muscles we will be dealing with today. In addition, the tensing procedure will make a vivid contrast between tension and relaxation and will give you an excellent opportunity to directly compare the two and appreciate the difference in feeling associated with each of these states.

Do you have any questions about what I've said so far? (Answer any questions about the rationale behind relaxation training but defer questions about specific procedures until after you have covered the material to follow.)

Now the purpose of this first session is to help you learn to become deeply relaxed, perhaps more relaxed than you've ever been before, and we can begin this session by going over the muscle groups that we're going to be dealing with in relaxation training. At this point in training, there are sixteen muscle groups to be dealt with, sixteen groups which are tensed and relaxed. As your skill develops, this number will be reduced significantly.

We will begin training with the hand and forearm (the therapist should ascertain which arm and hand are dominant and begin on that side; for most clients this will be the right hand and right lower arm). I'll ask you to tense the muscles in the right hand and right lower arm by making a tight fist. Now you should be able to feel tension in the hand, over the knuckles, and up into the lower arm. Can you feel that tension? O.K., fine. After we've relaxed that group of muscles we will then move to the muscles of the right biceps, and I'll ask you to tense these muscles by pushing your elbow down against the arm of the chair. You should be able to get a feeling of tension in the biceps without involving the muscles in the lower arm and hand. O.K., can you feel tension there now? (Several muscle groups may be tensed through alternative strategies and these are covered in the next section of this chapter.) All right, now after we've completed the relaxation of the right hand and lower arm and the right biceps, we'll move over to the muscles of the left hand and left lower arm and tense and relax them in the same way as we did on the right side. We'll also tense and relax the muscles of the left biceps just as we did the right biceps.

After we've relaxed the arms and hands, we'll relax the muscles of the face, and for conceptual purposes we're going to divide the facial muscles into 3 groups: first the muscles in the forehead area (the upper part of the face), then the muscles in the central part of the face (the upper part of the cheeks and the nose), and finally the lower part of the face (the jaws and the lower part of the cheeks). We'll begin with the muscles in the upper part of the face, and I'll ask you to tense these muscles by lifting the eyebrows just as high as you can and getting tension in the forehead and up into the scalp region. Can you feel that tension now? (At this point the therapist might want to make some statement about the fact that this part of the procedure involves a bit of face-making but that this is all part of the procedure; to further reassure the client the therapist himself should model the tensing strategies and thus make faces along with the client.)

O.K., fine. Now we'll move down to the muscles in the central part of the face and in order to tense these muscles I'll ask you to squint your eyes very tightly and at the same time wrinkle up your nose and get tension through the central part of the face. Can you feel the tension there in the upper part of the cheeks and through the eyes now? O.K., good. Next we'll tense the muscles in the lower part of the face and to do this I'll ask you to bite your teeth together and pull the corners of your mouth back. You should feel tension all through the lower part of the face and the jaw. Can you feel the tension in this area now?

Fine. After we've completed the facial muscles we'll move on to relax the muscles of the neck and in order to do this I'm going to ask you to pull your chin downward toward your chest and at the same time try to prevent it from actually touching the chest. That is, I want you to *counterpose* the muscles in the front part of the neck against those of the back part of the neck. You should feel just a little bit of shaking or trembling in these muscles as you tense them. Can you feel that now?

O.K., fine. We'll then move to the muscles of the chest, the shoulder and the upper back. We're going to combine quite a few muscles here and I'll ask you to tense these muscles by taking a deep breath, holding it, and at the same time pulling the shoulder blades together; that is, pull the shoulders back and try to make the shoulder blades touch. You should feel significant tension in the chest, the shoulders, and the upper back. Can you feel this tension now? O.K., fine.

Now we'll move on to the muscles of the abdomen and in order to tense the muscles in this region, I'm going to ask you to make your stomach hard; just tense it up as though you were going to hit yourself in the stomach. You should feel a good deal of tension and tightness in the stomach area now. Can you feel that tension? O.K., fine.

After relaxing the muscles in the stomach area, we'll then move on to the muscles of the legs and feet, and we'll begin with the right upper leg, the right thigh, and I'll ask you to tense the muscles of the right upper leg by counterposing the one large muscle on top of the leg with the two smaller ones underneath; you should be able to feel that large muscle on top get quite hard. Can you feel that now? O.K., good.

Then we'll move on to the muscles of the right calf, the right lower leg, and I'll ask you to tense the muscles here by pulling the toes upward toward your head. You should be able to feel tension all through the calf area. Can you feel that tension now? O.K., fine. Then we'll move on and tense the muscles of the right foot, and in order to do this I'll ask you to point the toe, turn the foot inward, and at the same time curl your toes. Now don't tense these muscles very hard, just enough to feel the tightness under the arch and in the ball of the foot. Can you feel that tension now? O.K., good.

We'll then move to the muscles of the left upper leg and tense and relax those muscles just as we did on the right side, then the muscles of the left lower leg, again using the same procedures as we used on the right side, and finally the left foot, tensing it and relaxing it just as we did on the other side.

Now do you have any specific questions about getting tension in any of the sixteen muscle groups that we've covered? (The therapist should at this point take time to assure that the client has been able to get tension in all the muscle groups covered and has understood how to produce this tension. Some clients may ask if they have to remember all of the tensing strategies and you should assure them that you will be repeating the means of getting tension in each group as you go through the first training session itself.)

O.K., fine. Now there are some points I would like to make about this procedure before we begin. I'm going to be asking you to pay very careful attention to the feelings of relaxation that appear in the various muscle groups and since we'll be starting with the right hand and the right lower arm I'm going to be using that as a reference point against which to compare the next muscle group. So, for example, when we're working on the right biceps I'll ask you a question like "Does the right biceps feel as relaxed as the right hand and right lower arm?" Thus as we go through this procedure I will be asking for comparative judgments on your part so that we can be assured that each muscle group gets as deeply relaxed as the one prior to it.

Another very important point to remember is that I will expect you to release the tension that you build up in these muscle groups immediately upon my cue. Please don't let the tension dissipate gradually. For example, when you have been tensing the muscles in the right hand and right lower arm, I'll ask you to relax, and when I do, I'd like you to completely and immediately release all the tension that's present in the right hand and lower arm. Do not gradually open the hand; let all the tension go at the same time.

Once we have relaxed a group of muscles there is some advantage in not moving that group of muscles. Thus, I'll ask you not to move in the chair unnecessarily; however, you may feel free to move in any way that helps you to continue to maintain a comfortable position at all times. Do not be afraid to move, but do not make any unnecessary movements during the session.

I'm also going to ask you not to talk to me

during this session; we will communicate by means of hand signals on your part. Thus, for example, I might ask you to signal if there is complete relaxation in the right hand and the right lower arm by lifting the little finger of your right hand (the hand signal should be made with the hand which is closest to the therapist). If the right hand and right lower arm felt completely relaxed you would then signal this to me just by lifting the little finger; if you felt that these muscles were not completely relaxed, there would be nothing for you to do. Not signaling would indicate to me that there was some tension still remaining.

I expect this first session will take us about 40-45 minutes to complete, so you might like to visit the restroom before we begin.

(If this proves unnecessary, or after it has been accomplished, the therapist should ask the client to remove any constraints such as watches or tight rings. The client should also remove eye glasses and be sure to check for the presence of contact lenses; these should also be removed before relaxation training.)

Now many of these procedures will become much clearer to you as we go through them, but do you have any further questions at this point? (The therapist should answer all pertinent questions at this point such that the client understands the procedures which are to come and is ready to begin training.) O.K., fine; now I'm going to ask you to recline in your chair to the fully reclined position and I will dim the lights in the room so that we can effectively cut down external stimulation. We can now begin. Just close your eyes, keep them closed throughout the session, and get into a good comfortable position in the chair.

ALTERNATIVE TENSING STRATEGIES

Many clients have some difficulty in achieving tension through the procedures outlined in the preceding section. Therefore, for several of these muscle groups some alternative tension strategies are available.

For those clients who have difficulty in getting tension in the biceps by pressing the elbow down against the chair, the therapist should ask the client to press the elbow down and at the same time pull the elbow inward toward the body. This usually will produce tension in the upper arm while leaving the lower arm and hand in a state of relaxation; the therapist should avoid having the client tense the biceps by lifting the lower arm and hand off the chair, that is, by bending the elbow. But if all else fails, this procedure can be employed (the order of tensing the arm muscles should be reversed, i.e. the muscles of the biceps should be tensed and relaxed prior to dealing with the muscles of the lower arm and hand). This should be used only in cases in which no other tensing strategy produces the desired results.

The muscles of the forehead can be tensed by asking the client to produce an exaggerated frown, that is, by "knitting the brows." This technique usually suffices if the original strategy of raising the eyebrows fails.

Clients who have difficulty producing tension in the neck through the *counterposition* (tensing two opposing sets of muscles simultaneously) of the muscles in the front and back of the neck can often achieve satisfactory results by pressing the head back against the chair, that is, by using their neck muscles to exert pressure against the chair. This is a less desirable means of tensing the neck muscles since it does not involve counterposition and one group of muscles or the other is likely to be left out of the procedure. However, it is a possible alternative.

An alternative means of tensing the muscles of the chest, shoulders, and upper back is for the client to imagine that two strings hanging from the ceiling and attached to his/her shoulders (like a puppet's strings) are being pulled upward. This should produce an exaggerated shrug of the shoulders *and* the desired tension.

There are two alternative strategies for getting tension in the abdominal region. Instead of asking the client to "make the stomach hard," the therapist can ask the client to either pull the stomach in as far as it will go or push the stomach outward. Neither of these procedures is as effective as the standard strategy which actually produces counterposition of muscles in the abdomen. One of these three techniques almost always succeeds.

For clients who find it difficult to produce tension in the thighs in the standard fashion, the therapist can suggest that the client lift the leg *very slightly*, thereby producing tension in the upper leg. Again this procedure is likely to involve only one set of muscles and is not recommended as standard procedure.

An alternative tensing procedure for the calves involves asking the client to point the toes away from the head rather than to pull the toes upward toward the head. This is a very good alternative strategy and will succeed with most clients who are unable to get tension with the standard procedure.

This list of alternatives is not exhaustive. The therapist may find that these alternatives may not succeed with a particular client's problem or that a client may have difficulty in getting tension in a group which has no alternative strategy in this list. In either of these cases the therapist must devise a strategy which will produce the desired tension in the problem muscle group.

At this point, the therapist's concern should not be with adhering to standard procedures but rather with creating an alternative through which the client can get tension. The client and therapist should work together (as they must throughout relaxation training) to solve any problems which exist. Failure to find solutions to such problems could have important implications for the success of the training program since the production of adequate tension is a necessary condition for the building of skill in relaxation.

Another problem with which the therapist may be confronted is that the client may feel a certain muscle group has not been dealt with. (For example, a client may state that, while the muscles of the upper back feel well relaxed after application of standard techniques, the muscles of the lower back remain tense.) This does not happen often, but if such a situation occurs, the therapist must develop a tensing strategy which allows the client to achieve relaxation in these muscles. This can best be accomplished by asking the client to tense the muscle group in any way he/she wants. The client should describe how the tension is produced so that the therapist can give appropriate tensing instructions at later sessions.

6   Session I: The Basic Procedures

After the client has understood and accepted the rationale underlying progressive relaxation training and after the therapist is assured that all of the client's questions have been satisfactorily answered, the actual relaxation training can begin. This training should follow the sequence outlined to the client during rationale presentation; that is, the sixteen muscle groups discussed and practiced with the client during the rationale should be covered in the initial training session itself. The sequence should be identical to the sequence used during rationale presentation, and the muscle tension procedures agreed upon with the client should be employed throughout. For example, if an alternative tensing procedure for the biceps was determined, then that same procedure should be employed in the training itself.

THE BASIC PROCEDURE

Recall that the order in which the muscle groups are dealt with is as follows:

1. Dominant hand and forearm
2. Dominant biceps
3. Nondominant hand and forearm
4. Nondominant biceps
5. Forehead
6. Upper cheeks and nose
7. Lower cheeks and jaws
8. Neck and throat
9. Chest, shoulders, and upper back
10. Abdominal or stomach region
11. Dominant thigh
12. Dominant calf
13. Dominant foot
14. Nondominant thigh
15. Nondominant calf
16. Nondominant foot

In teaching relaxation to a client, there is a succession of events which must occur with respect to each muscle group. The sequence is as follows:

1. The client's attention should be focused on the muscle group.
2. At a predetermined signal from the therapist, the muscle group is tensed.
3. Tension is maintained for a period of 5-7 seconds (this duration is shorter in the case of the feet).
4. At a predetermined cue, the muscle group is released.
5. The client's attention is maintained upon the muscle group as it relaxes.

DIRECTING THE PROCEDURE

The therapist can easily direct this sequence of events by employing a relatively standard set of directional statements. (Most of the following material is illustrated on the record which accompanies this manual.) In order to accomplish the first step in the sequence outlined above, the therapist should say, for example, "O.K., now I'd like you to focus all of your attention on the muscles of your right hand and lower arm."

Once the first step is accomplished, the therapist can direct precise onset of the tension cycle by saying, for example, "Alright, by making a tight fist I'd like you to tense the muscles in the right hand and lower arm, *now*." Notice that the tensing statement includes an instruction as to how to achieve tension and a reminder of which group the client is to focus on. The client should not actually begin tensing until the therapist says "Now," and thus the client should be made aware of the fact that the word "Now" is the tension cue. Having a specific tension signal is important because the therapist needs to accurately time the exact length of tension; the client should not be allowed to begin tensing randomly.

The third step in the sequence consists simply of having the client hold the tension for 5-7 seconds. During this interval the therapist should be aiding the client in focusing on the feelings associated with tension by making statements like "Feel the muscles pull; notice what it's like to feel tension in these muscles as they pull and remain hard and tight." The therapist should restrict the amount of this verbal behavior so that it coincides with the length of the tensing period and not, in the interest of making three or four statements during the tension period, extend the period beyond about 7 seconds. It is important that the therapist keep the client's attention focused upon the feelings associated with tension.

The therapist should terminate the tension period with a standard statement like "O.K., relax." At this point the muscle group is released, and the therapist must keep the client's attention focused on the feelings in the muscle group as it relaxes. To achieve this, the therapist would, for 30-40 seconds, make statements to the client designed to focus attention on the relaxation process as it is occurring. These statements should be such that the therapist merely points out to the client what is happening. Thus, the client should be made a passive and careful observer of these processes.

The statements made by the therapist should therefore be suggestive, not prescriptive. For example, immediately after the word "Relax," the therapist could say, "Just let these muscles go, noticing the difference between tension and relaxation, focusing on the feeling in this muscle group as it becomes more and more relaxed." (A full presentation of the kinds of statements which can be made at this point in the procedure is available in Appendix B.)

The therapist should at all times avoid making direct suggestions or prescriptive statements such as "Relax these muscles more and more," or "These muscles are becoming more and more relaxed now." There are two reasons for this word of caution. First, the use of direct suggestion may result in the production of hypnosis-like phenomena in the session. This is to be avoided for reasons discussed in Chapter 11. Secondly,

direct suggestions may very well be at variance with what is going on from the client's point of view. Thus, if a given muscle group is not relaxed and the therapist is making statements like "These muscles are deeply and completely relaxed," the client will either fear that his/her own performance was inadequate or believe that the therapist is incompetent. While we would prefer our clients not to think of us as incompetent therapists, even that is preferable to a client feeling incompetent or inadequate. This anxiety would disrupt the state of relaxation which the therapist is attempting to initiate. Thus the verbal behavior on the part of the therapist during the relaxation periods should consist of indirect statements designed to encourage the client to focus attention on the muscle group being relaxed.

After the 30-40 seconds of relaxation "patter," the tension-release sequence is repeated; that is, the therapist says, for example, "O.K., again I'd like you to tense the muscles in the right hand and lower arm, now." After 5-7 seconds of tension, the client is instructed to relax and again hears indirect statements about relaxation and giving attention to relaxation, this time for 45-60 seconds. As relaxation training with a given client progresses, it is often true that the second tension-release cycle is unnecessary to achieve the desired degree of relaxation. However, it is usually a good idea to repeat the cycle since the result will generally be even further reduction of tension in that muscle group. Also, the client may not know what deep relaxation feels like and might think that a group is completely relaxed when actually it is not as deeply relaxed as it will be after a second tension-release cycle.

ASSURING COMPLETE RELAXATION

Thus, each of the sixteen muscle groups is tensed and relaxed twice. Before moving on to the next muscle group, however, the therapist must determine that deep local relaxation has, in fact, been achieved. This is best accomplished by the use of the hand signal agreed upon during the rationale presentation. After the 45-60 seconds of relaxation following the second tension cycle, the therapist should say, for example, "Alright, if the muscles in the right hand and right lower arm feel completely relaxed, I'd like you to signal by lifting the little finger on the right hand." (Again notice that the signaling hand is the one closer to the therapist.) For all but the initial hand and forearm group, this should be a statement such as "If the muscles of ------------ are as deeply relaxed as the muscles of ------------, please signal to me." The intergroup comparisons are as follows:

1. The dominant biceps to the dominant hand and forearm
2. The nondominant hand and forearm to the dominant hand and forearm
3. The nondominant biceps to the nondominant hand and forearm
4. The forehead to the nondominant biceps
5. The central section of the face to the forehead
6. The lower part of the face to the central part of the face
7. The neck to all facial muscles
8. The chest, shoulders, and back to the neck
9. The abdomen to the chest
10. The dominant upper leg to the abdomen
11. The dominant lower leg to the dominant upper leg
12. The dominant foot to the dominant lower leg
13. The nondominant upper leg to the dominant upper leg
14. The nondominant lower leg to the nondominant upper leg
15. The nondominant foot to the nondominant lower leg

Later in training (see Chapter 7) when fewer muscle groups are employed, each group should be compared to the one immediately preceding it.

If the client signals, thus indicating that the group in question is completely relaxed (or as relaxed as the group to which it is compared), the therapist might say, "Alright, fine, just allow these muscles to go right on relaxing while you shift all of your attention to the next muscle group, the right biceps." Then the entire procedure is repeated with the next group. It is seldom

true, however, early in training especially, that a client will signal complete relaxation every time this information is requested. In fact, a therapist who receives a signal of complete relaxation every time during a first session should suspect that the client may be an extremely acquiescent subject who may not be relaxed but is in some sense afraid to "give the therapist any trouble." The therapist can usually determine the presence of this acquiescence through the questioning which occurs after the first session (these questions will be covered later in this chapter).

In addition to these questions there are some fairly obvious nonverbal clues given by the client to the therapist. If a client is signaling complete relaxation in every muscle group and at the same time is fidgeting in the chair, does not have slow and regular breathing, often opens his/her eyes, attempts to talk to the therapist, or displays other nonrelaxed behaviors, the therapist should be unimpressed with the relaxation signals being made. During the session this problem may be alleviated by making some statement like "Please be sure not to signal relaxation unless you really feel deeply relaxed in the group in question." The client should also be reminded that it is acceptable to signal the absence of relaxation (i.e. to fail to signal relaxation) and that the client should not be concerned with possibly disappointing the therapist. The client should realize that the goal of the session is to produce a very relaxed experience, not to "go through the motions" of relaxing. (These problems and many others are considered in some detail in Chapter 9.)

In case of failure to get a relaxation signal after going through two tension-release cycles, the standard procedure is simply to repeat the tension-release cycle. Refocus attention, ask the client to tense the muscle group for 5-7 seconds and again relax, and go through 45-60 seconds of indirect relaxation suggestions. At this point another signal for relaxation can be requested. This procedure usually is ultimately successful, but it should not be repeated an infinite number of times. Thus, if a client is still not signaling relaxation after the muscle group has been tensed 4-5 times, the therapist should attempt an alternative solution to the problem (see Chapter 9). Further extension of the procedure is ill-advised because it may cause client fatigue or even pain in the muscle group being tensed.

TWO CHANGES IN PROCEDURE

If there are no serious difficulties in achieving relaxation in any particular group, the training session continues. With two exceptions, the procedure is unaltered for each of the sixteen groups. First, as noted earlier, the muscles of the feet should not be tensed much longer than about 5 seconds due to the danger of cramping. The possibility of cramping should not be communicated directly to the client since such a communication might cause unnecessary anxiety. The tension period should be shortened for any muscle group which cramps easily for the particular client. For example, if a client has difficulty with cramps in the calves, the therapist should shorten the tension cycle for this group and may even suggest that the client not tense this group quite as hard as the others. The client should be informed that the tension cycle will be shortened and that this will eliminate the cramping problem.

The other change in the standard relaxation training procedure occurs while the muscles of the chest, shoulders, and upper back are being relaxed. At this point, two changes are introduced into the therapist's verbal behavior. The first of these is that "breathing cues" are added to the indirect suggestions following tension. That is, starting with the chest muscle group through all the remaining groups, the therapist can introduce indirect suggestions about breathing into the "patter." Thus after allowing a group of muscles to relax, the therapist might say, "Noticing the slow and regular breathing." The therapist can also begin pacing the rhythm of the verbal suggestions to coincide with the client's breathing.

The second change in the therapist's verbal behavior involves asking that the client take a deep breath and hold it upon tensing each of the muscle groups which follow the chest, shoulders, and upper back. Thus the client should be told that from this point

on, "I will be asking you to take a deep breath and hold it as you tense each muscle group and to let that breath out as you release the tension." This changes the therapist's statement with respect to initiating tension. After focusing the client's attention on, for example, the abdomen, the therapist should say, "O.K., by taking a deep breath and making these muscles hard, I'd like you to tense the muscles in the abdominal region *now*." Notice that we have simply added the instruction to take a deep breath in order to remind the client to follow the new procedure. This "breath-holding" technique has at least two distinct advantages. First, it associates the release of breath with feelings of relaxation, and this can be quite helpful in learning deep relaxation, especially when practicing at home. Second, it is likely to insure very deep relaxation of the chest and the abdominal region. These regions are usually, if not always, associated with the kinds of tension individuals experience in various real-life situations, and thus it is very important to insure that the client has considerable skill in relaxing these areas.

SUMMARY AND ASSESSMENT

After the client has signaled relaxation for all sixteen muscle groups, the therapist is ready to make a final assessment of the client's state of relaxation. The therapist should give a report of the muscles which have been relaxed and an instruction to allow them to continue relaxing. This is accomplished by saying, for example, "O.K., now, we've relaxed the muscles in the arms and hands; just allow them to continue relaxing. We've relaxed the muscles in the face and neck; go on allowing them to remain deeply relaxed. We've relaxed the muscles of the chest, the shoulders, the upper back, the abdomen; allow these muscles now to become even more deeply relaxed. We've relaxed the muscles of the legs and feet; just allow these muscles now to remain deeply and completely relaxed."

When the summary has been completed, the therapist can easily assess the client's state of relaxation by asking as follows: "Now I would like you to signal if you feel the slightest bit of tension in any muscle group anywhere in the body." If the client does not signal, this is an indication that he/she is completely relaxed all through the body. At this point the therapist may want to make certain that the client has heard the question by asking a supplementary question such as, "O.K., I'd like you to signal if you feel completely relaxed all through the body." If the client signals at this point, the therapist has confirmation of the client's state of relaxation and can terminate the session according to the procedures outlined below.

If the client does not indicate complete relaxation at this point, the therapist is faced with the task of locating any remaining tension and eliminating it. This can be done relatively easily by informing the client that the sixteen muscle groups of the body will be named and that he/she should signal at the mention of a muscle group which has not achieved complete relaxation. At this point, the therapist should begin to slowly list the muscle groups. Whenever the client signals, indicating that tension is present in the muscle group, the therapist should take note of this and then ask the client to signal if there is tension in any other muscle group in the body. If there is a signal at this point, the therapist must continue until any tension still present in the body has been specified; otherwise, the only tension present has already been detected.

Once the trouble has been localized, the corrective procedures are exactly those outlined previously; that is, the group can be tensed and relaxed once again. This usually will eliminate any residual tension which has built up over the course of the session. (The presence of tension does not always mean that the group was never relaxed. Clients will often report the return of some tension in a muscle group that had been relaxed at one point.) The therapist should direct two more standard tension-release cycles before attempting an alternative tensing strategy.

The therapist should obtain a signal from the client that the group is indeed now completely relaxed, then repeat the original assessment question; that is, "I'd like a signal now if you feel any tension anywhere throughout the body."

When the therapist is assured that no residual tension exists anywhere in the body, the session can be terminated. Prior to termination, however, it is advisable to allow the client a minute or two to enjoy this state of complete relaxation. During this period the therapist may either remain silent or make, at 15-20 second intervals, indirect suggestions designed to keep the client's attention focused upon the very pleasant state of relaxation. These suggestions should remind the client to pay attention to what it feels like to be completely and deeply relaxed.

TERMINATING RELAXATION

After this "enjoyment period" the therapist is ready to terminate the session. The client should be informed that the therapist will count backward from 4 to 1 and that on the count of 4 the client should begin to move legs and feet, on the count of 3 move arms and hands, on the count of 2 move head and neck, and on the count of 1 the client should open his/her eyes. The therapist should include in this information some suggestion of the feeling of well-being and relaxation, for example, "Then on the count of 1 I'll ask you to open your eyes, feeling quite calm and relaxed, very pleasantly relaxed, just as if you'd had a brief nap." This remark about a brief nap is very helpful in the sense that many clients "awake" after an initial session feeling somewhat dizzy and disoriented since they have never before experienced the depth of relaxation achieved in this first session. Arousal from deep relaxation is similar to waking up, and therefore this statement at the end of the termination instruction can help to allay any concerns that the client might have about these feelings.

POST-RELAXATION QUESTIONING

At this point the therapist should ask a very important group of post-session questions. These should be asked in a somewhat structured fashion, and the therapist should give careful attention to the answers. The therapist should first ask an open-ended question like "How do you feel?" or "Well, how was that?" or "How did you like that?" The client's answer to this question should be an overall reaction to the procedure itself and may contain a variety of general statements. At this point the therapist should begin collecting more detailed information by asking specific questions about any problems that occurred during the session, for example, "What was the trouble in getting the neck muscles relaxed?"

In this way, the therapist can explore with the client any areas in which relaxation was not routine. If the entire procedure was relatively routine, then the therapist can ask a more general question such as "I'd like you to think back over this session and tell me if you at any time had any problems getting the various muscle groups relaxed." The client is then likely to mention some problems or questions that he/she might have had that did not get communicated to the therapist during the session.

Whether problems are brought up by the client spontaneously or uncovered by the therapist in this questioning, it is important that some resolution of the problems is agreed upon. If an alternative tensing strategy is required, this should be determined; if there is a point that the therapist did not communicate adequately to the client, this should be clarified. The point of delineating these concerns is to provide a list of problems to be eliminated so that the relaxation procedure can become routine and trouble-free. (We have tried to include in Chapter 9 all of the problems which have arisen in our past experience, but there is no guarantee that an unusual problem will not be encountered by the reader; the therapist must create a unique and original solution to such a problem.)

During this problem resolution period, the therapist should at all times maintain an air of confidence. Problems should be dealt with in a very routine fashion. The therapist should indicate that these kinds of difficulties have occurred before and that there are corrective procedures available. He/she should then assure the client that the problems will in all probability disappear as the client practices the new procedures.

After any problems which arose during the session have been discussed and resolved, the therapist can ask the client to describe, in his/her own words, what relaxation feels like. This account is quite important because it helps the therapist to understand the kinds of sensations being experienced by this particular client and can aid the therapist in adapting the "patter" to that client. For example, if in describing how relaxation feels, the client says that his/her limbs felt lighter or that he/she began to feel somewhat warmer or cooler, the therapist should note this information and include it in later sessions as part of the indirect suggestions. In the case of a client who experiences a warm feeling and heaviness in the limbs, the therapist could in subsequent sessions say, "Noticing the warm, heavy feelings of relaxation flowing into these muscles now as they become more relaxed." The therapist can thus avoid making statements or indirect suggestions which are in fact not appropriate for a given client. Such information should be recorded carefully and referred to during subsequent sessions.

The therapist should also ask at this point if anything that was said during the initial session made it more difficult for the client to relax. If the client mentions any such statements, they should of course be eliminated from future sessions. A therapist should also ask if there were any statements made which facilitated the client's relaxation, and these should be emphasized in subsequent sessions.

ASSIGNING HOME PRACTICE

When the information regarding problems seems to be complete and when the therapist knows better what to say in future sessions, the initial session is brought to a close by providing the client with a description of the practice procedure to be followed, i.e. the "homework assignment." The importance of practicing cannot be overemphasized to the client; the therapist should repeat the learning analogy, making it clear that relaxation is a skill which must be practiced if it is to improve. The client should be encouraged to practice *every day, twice a day*, for periods of about 15-20 minutes each time, with at least three hours separating the two daily practice sessions.

The client may ask how the practice session can be so short when the initial session was so lengthy. The therapist should make it clear that there are two reasons why this is so: (1) the initial session was an introduction to the procedure, and, with practice, the client will be able to attain deep relaxation in shorter periods of time, and (2) the client can focus more closely on the sensations in his/her own body and direct a more efficient pacing of the practice. Much of the slower pacing imposed by the therapist is not needed to achieve relaxation, and most clients, even early in training, do find 15-20 minutes is more than adequate. The therapist and client should also discuss in detail the client's home situation and decide on a physical setting for the practice. Since most clients do not have plush reclining chairs, several alternatives, such as a bed, are possible. The client should simply lie down on the bed with his/her head on a pillow. Another alternative would be a large, overstuffed chair with a footstool. This would be perfectly appropriate if it is comfortable for the client. If neither of these solutions is feasible, the therapist should find some alternative arrangement which will provide a comfortable location for relaxation practice.

There are several conditions for successful home practicing. First, as has been stated, an appropriate chair or bed must be located. Second, the client must practice where interruption by other people, telephones, doorbells, etc. is unlikely. Meeting this requirement may involve considerable planning on the part of the client and the therapist. Finally, the client should be cautioned to practice relaxation only at those times of the day when there is no time pressure; for instance, practicing should *not* take place 15-20 minutes before the client has an appointment.

The ideal practice situation would be one in which the client has nothing to do for a reasonably long period of time and can focus full attention on relaxation practice. While quiet times of the day vary for different people, it is often helpful to suggest such times as after work, just after dinner, or just before retiring at night. But satisfying the requirements listed above should take precedence over reserving any particular time of day.

The client must be motivated to practice. The therapist should use all of his/her clinical skills to encourage regular practice and not be particularly tolerant of the client's excuses for not practicing. The therapist should remind the client that failing to practice has serious implications for the speed with which skill in relaxation will be learned.

THE THERAPIST'S VOICE

In progressive relaxation training, *how* the therapist says what he/she says is just as important as *what* is actually said. Subtle features of volume and inflection are of vital importance in the adequate presentation of these procedures to the client and it is for this reason that the record which accompanies this manual has been produced.

The therapist should begin the first relaxation session in a conversational tone, i.e. at the same level of volume used in the rationale presentation. Over the course of this first session, however, the therapist's voice should show a progressive reduction in volume consistent with the progressive increase in relaxation in the client. However, at no time should the therapist speak so softly that the client would have difficulty in hearing the instructions given. The therapist should be careful not to introduce hypnotic or seductive components into the voice quality; rather, the tone should be smooth and quiet, perhaps even monotonous, but not purposely hypnotic. In addition to speaking more softly as the session progresses, the pace of speech should be reduced so that the therapist is speaking considerably more slowly by the time the relaxation session is one-half to two-thirds completed. The changes in speed, tone, and inflection are very subtle and are best illustrated by the accompanying record.

The Tension-Release Voice Cycle

Within the overall reduction of volume and speed in the therapist's voice, there should be a cyclical aspect based on the content of the speech. That is, the therapist's voice should sound quite different during instructions to tense muscle groups than during indirect suggestions of relaxation and attention focusing. As the therapist gives the signal to tense a muscle group, his/her voice should increase in volume, speed, and tension. This should be clearly perceptible to the client and is best achieved by the therapist's actually tensing a muscle group in his/her own body (perhaps the most convenient group for this purpose would be the dominant hand and lower arm). This tension should be reflected in voice quality. At the point of giving the cue to relax, the therapist's voice should again change. He/she should release the tension in the muscle group and in the voice and perhaps even exhale in coincidence with the relaxation cue. That is, exhaling occurs at the cue word "Relax." There should be a very sharp division between the end of the tension period and the beginning of the relaxation period, not only in terms of the instructions but in terms of the sound of the therapist's voice. The difference aids the client in distinguishing between relaxation and tension.

Some Words of Warning

At no time during the session should the therapist's voice take on overly dramatic or theatrical qualities. Rather, it should be used as an instrument for facilitating the relaxation process. The client's reaction to both voice quality and the content of the therapist's speech should be discussed during the post-session question period. The therapist should take some precautions to insure that there was nothing in the quality of his/her voice which was disruptive to the client; the therapist should not be satisfied with the assurance that the content was adequate.

In Chapter 5 the reader was cautioned not to memorize a speech to be used during rationale presentation. The same caution is offered here; while we hope that the record accompanying this manual will be of considerable illustrative benefit, we do not feel that it is appropriate for the reader to attempt to precisely imitate the verbal behavior of the therapist on the record. Thus, while we do feel that it is helpful to follow the general rules and procedures associated with voice quality, speed, etc., this must be done within the context of the reader's own style of speaking. The important thing is that the therapist sound natural, confident, competent. It is *not* important that the therapist sound precisely like the demonstration record.

7 Variations on the Basic Procedures

Once the client is capable of achieving deep relaxation with tension-release cycles in sixteen muscle groups, the therapist can begin instituting a series of procedures designed to decrease the amount of time and physical exertion necessary to achieve deep relaxation. The sequence begins with procedures designed to ultimately decrease to four the number of muscle groups involved in relaxation. Following successful completion of that section of the program, the therapist will introduce a procedure known as *recall*. In the recall procedure, actual tensing of muscles is eliminated and the client learns to remember the feelings associated with tension and release. Control over muscle tension will be quite extensive at this stage and the production of actual muscle tension is no longer necessary. After the recall procedure has been mastered, relaxation begins to occur throughout the entire body rather than in specific muscle groups, and the final step in the program outlined in this chapter is teaching the client to achieve deep relaxation through the use of a counting procedure which requires neither muscular tension nor recall procedures.

There are many advantages to a technique by which the client can voluntarily control tension and produce relaxation all through the body without performing any observable exertion. The most obvious of advantages is that the client can employ relaxation techniques even when reclining in a chair with eyes closed would be impractical. Relaxation thus becomes a skill which the client can "carry around" and use in any troublesome situation. This skill can be especially helpful when the client is entering an unfamiliar situation; having a tool which can be employed to ease any tension which might arise can greatly increase his/her confidence. The recall and counting procedures are an integral part of a technique known as *differential relaxation*, which is discussed more fully in Chapter 8.

RELAXATION PROCEDURES FOR SEVEN MUSCLE GROUPS

In this procedure, as in those to follow, the most important consideration is that the client be fully informed about any forthcoming changes in procedure. The therapist should familiarize the client with the combined muscle groups which will be employed in the seven-group procedure. The original sixteen groups are combined as follows:

(1)   The muscles of the dominant arm are tensed and relaxed as a single group; thus the hand, lower arm, and biceps muscles are combined. The means of achieving tension throughout the arm and hand can vary from client to client; perhaps the easiest procedure is to ask the client to hold the arm out in front of him/her with the elbow bent at about 45 degrees and make a fist, thus tensing not only the muscles of the hand and lower arm, but also the biceps at the same time. An alternative to this would be to have the client leave his/her arm supported on the arm of the chair and, while bending the arm at the elbow, make a fist and press the elbow down and/or in. Of course, any alternative tensing strategy which produces the desired tension may be used; these alternatives have been outlined because they have proved successful in the past.

(2)   The muscles of the nondominant arm constitute the second group and are tensed and relaxed in the same way as was group 1.

(3)   The next group in the sequence combines the three formerly separate facial muscle groups. These are combined into one group by asking the client to perform simultaneously all of the three tension procedures previously employed separately. Thus the client should be asked to raise the eyebrows (or frown), squint the eyes, wrinkle up the nose, bite down, and pull the corners of the mouth back. This should produce tension all through the facial area. (Some clients may at first

have difficulty in combining some of these groups; they should be encouraged to practice the combinations and the therapist should insure that the particular tensing strategy employed is maximally efficient since this will increase the probability of learning the new skills.)

(4)   The fourth muscle group is identical to the group employed in the sixteen-group procedure: the neck and throat. This group is tensed just as before.

(5)   The fifth muscle group involves combination of the chest, shoulders, upper back, and abdomen. To achieve tension, the client should be asked to take a deep breath, hold it, and pull the shoulder blades back and together, while at the same time making the stomach hard (or pulling it in or pushing it out).

(6)   The muscles of the dominant thigh, calf, and foot constitute the sixth group of muscles; in order to pro-duce tension here, the client should be asked to lift the leg off the chair very slightly while pointing the toes and turning the foot inward. Again, this may be difficult at first, and the client may have to experiment to ascertain the best procedure for getting adequate tension. Any procedure is acceptable as long as the client does report tension throughout the entire area.

(7)   The procedure employed for the seventh group (the nondominant thigh, calf, and foot) is identical to that used for group 6.

At the conclusion of the first session in which seven groups have been employed, the therapist should question the client to uncover any particular problems that might have occurred. This question period should be a shortened version of the one held after the first training session. The therapist should be certain after this first seven-group session that the procedure is clear and that tension was achieved in all groups without particular difficulty. It is also most important to determine that the depth of relaxation was satisfactory to the client.

During the first session with a reduced number of muscle groups, the client may report that relaxation was not quite as satisfactory as had been the case in the more familiar sixteen-group procedure. This should not be cause for alarm, however; the therapist should simply ask the client to practice at home, using the shortened procedure, and report at the next session whether it has resulted in increased relaxation efficiency. A week of practice will usually result in a satisfactory report on this question. As the therapist guides the client through these more abbreviated procedures, mastery of them will take practice, just as the original procedure did. Therefore, there may be slight setbacks at each transition point in the relaxation training program, and the therapist should be prepared for such occurrences. The client's verbal report should, however, indicate that overall progress is continuing and that the procedure is becoming more efficient all the time. If after two or three weeks the client continues to report less relaxation than with the sixteen-group procedure, the therapist should ascertain which muscle groups are not becoming well relaxed. The components of these groups may have to be practiced individually before reinstituting the use of the combined groups.

RELAXATION PROCEDURES FOR FOUR MUSCLE GROUPS

This procedure represents a further condensation of procedures already employed. The groups are combined as follows:

(1)   The first of the four groups consists of the muscles of the left and right arms, hands, and biceps. They are combined into one group and are tensed at the same time simply by asking the client to combine whatever tensing strategies he/she had been using for each arm separately. This may mean that the client is either lifting both arms off the chair and bending them at the elbows or resting them on the chair and making a fist in both hands.

(2)   The second group is made up of the muscles of the face and neck. In order to get tension throughout this area, the client should be asked to tense all of the facial muscles while at the same time employing the tension procedure for the neck. This should produce adequate results, including the trembling which is characteristic of tension in the neck region.

(3)   The third muscle group in this procedure includes the muscles of the chest, shoulders, back, and abdomen.

There is no change from the seven-group stage.

(4)   The final group to be tensed in this procedure consists of the muscles of both the left and right upper leg, calf, and foot, and again requires that the client simply combine the tension procedures he had been using in tensing each leg separately. This procedure usually can be mastered with little difficulty. However problems sometimes result from the use of inappropriate chairs. If there is any danger that tensing both legs at the same time will cause the client to lose balance and slip out of the chair, the therapist should remain at the previous seven-group level; that is, he should allow the client to continue tensing one leg at a time, thus creating a five-group technique.

Once the client has learned to achieve deep relaxation using four muscle groups, the relaxation procedure should last less than ten minutes. While this represents considerable savings in time for both the therapist and the client, the procedures outlined in this section are not designed simply to allow relaxation to occur more quickly. The therapist should not be intent on setting speed records. The major goal is development of the client's ability to easily achieve deep relaxation at any time. The fact that this can occur rapidly is a secondary benefit. If the therapist has inadvertently placed an emphasis on speed, there may be difficulty in moving to the recall procedure since the client will have too little time to focus closely enough upon the feelings associated with relaxation.

RELAXATION THROUGH RECALL

The recall procedure differs quite markedly from all of the preceding procedures in that it does not require the client to exert muscular tension. It does require full use of the client's increased ability to focus on tension and relaxation. Before beginning the initial recall session the client should be fully informed about the procedures to come. The therapist should be certain that the client understands these procedures and is ready to attempt them.

Relaxation with recall employs the same four muscle groups which had been employed in the previous procedure: i.e. both arms as the first group; face and neck as the second; chest, shoulders, back, and stomach as the third; and legs and feet as the fourth.

In this procedure, the therapist need only provide for two sequential events: first, the careful focusing of the client's attention on any tension in a particular muscle group, and second, the instruction to the client to recall the feelings associated with release of that tension. In order to help the client focus attention the therapist could say, "O.K., now I'd like you to focus all your attention on the muscles of the arms and hands and very carefully identify any feelings of tightness or tension that might be present there now. Notice where this tension is and what it feels like."

Following the focusing of attention, the therapist can go directly into the relaxation mode by saying, for example, "O.K., and relax, just recalling what it was like when you released these muscles, just letting them go and allowing them to become more and more deeply relaxed." The therapist should continue the indirect suggestion "patter" for about 30-45 seconds. Thus, this procedure is analogous to the tension-release system, the only difference being that the actual production of tension is eliminated. At the conclusion of the 30-45 seconds of indirect relaxation suggestion the therapist should ask for a signal from the client if the particular muscle group feels completely relaxed. If the client signals, the therapist should continue to the next muscle group. If the signal is not forthcoming, the therapist should say, for example, "O.K., again I'd like you to focus all your attention on the muscles of the arms and hands, this time very carefully identifying where the residual tension is, focusing all of your attention on it, noticing what it feels like." The therapist should then give the relaxation cue and another 30-45 seconds of indirect suggestions involving focused recall of relaxation.

If serious trouble is encountered in getting a particular muscle group relaxed the therapist should employ the earlier procedure of tensing the muscle group. The therapist should, however, continue to attempt to use recall on all other muscle groups, and in fact should encourage the client to use recall on *all* groups in home practice sessions. The client should be led to expect that practicing will increase his/her skill with the recall procedure and that initial difficulties will be overcome; this expectation is almost always fulfilled.

With the exception of elimination of the actual tension production, this procedure is in other respects identical (e.g. in terms of final assessment and termination procedure) to the earlier stages of training.

RELAXATION BY RECALL WITH COUNTING

Once the client has learned to achieve deep relaxation through use of the recall procedure, the therapist can in sessions with the client add a counting procedure which the client can use later in home practice sessions. This counting procedure is included at the end of a successful recall session, just prior to termination of that session, but after assurance that complete relaxation has been achieved. At this time the therapist should inform the client that he/she is going to institute a procedure designed to allow relaxation to become even deeper. The therapist might say, "As you remain very deeply and completely relaxed now, I'm going to count from one to ten, and, as I count, I'd like you to allow all the muscles all through the body to become even more deeply and more completely relaxed on each count. Just focus your attention on all the muscles in the body and notice them as they become even more and more deeply relaxed as I count from one to ten." The therapist can then begin counting, interjecting indirect relaxation suggestions somewhat as follows: "One, two, noticing the arms and hands becoming more and more relaxed now; three, four, focusing on the muscles of the face and neck as they become even more deeply relaxed now; five, six, allowing the muscles in the chest, shoulders, back, and abdomen to relax even more deeply now; seven, eight, noticing the muscles of the legs and feet becoming more and more completely relaxed; nine, and ten." The therapist should pace this counting to coincide with the client's exhalations. Thus the counting speed would be much slower with clients who are more deeply relaxed and breathing more slowly. It is important to coordinate

counting with breathing since this will help the client use the same procedures in practicing at home.

Of course, as in all cases in the past, the use of this procedure should be fully outlined to the client before it is first used. He/she should be informed that this is a procedure designed to further focus attention and to allow the relaxation to become even more comfortable. It should not be referred to as a "deepening" procedure since this has some undesirable connotations involving hypnosis (see Chapter 11). After the initial use of the counting procedure the client should be encouraged to regularly employ counting at the conclusion of recall practicing and to report on its usefulness at home.

RELAXATION BY COUNTING ALONE

Once the client has successfully integrated the counting procedure into home practice sessions and the therapist is reasonably certain that it has become associated with deep relaxation, a procedure which consists solely of the therapist counting from one to ten and giving indirect suggestions of relaxation can be attempted. This technique is of primary usefulness as a time-saving device in the office setting, but some clients find it helpful in facing real-life stress situations. (Counting from one to ten has long been a technique for controlling anger; its usefulness is augmented through relaxation training.) Again, the therapist should explain to the client what the procedure will involve and allow the client to ask questions prior to initiating this session. The counting procedure can be identical to the one employed in the recall with counting procedure and should be followed by the usual assessment of relaxation. If at the end of the counting procedure the client indicates that some tension remains, the therapist should locate the residual tension and have the client remove it through the recall technique or, in case that should fail, through tension and release. In most cases, any reported residual tension is removable through the now well-established technique of recall.

The client can now attain deep and complete relaxation in a minute or less, depending upon the counting rate, and relaxation is a well-established skill which can be used in a variety of ways, some of which were mentioned in Chapter 3.

The client should be encouraged to continue practicing on a regular basis. For a client who is able to achieve deep relaxation by simply counting or through rapid recall, two relaxation practice sessions a day may be unnecessary; one may be quite enough to maintain skill at an adequate level. The client and therapist together should determine the proper amount of practice on the basis of the level of skill desired and the intended future use of relaxation skills. If, for example, relaxation is being used primarily as a means of relieving insomnia, practice sessions may be unnecessary since the client is employing relaxation skill at least once a day anyway. Other uses of the training may require more intensive practice.

We are dealing with a learned skill, not a magic wand. Therefore, some provision for continued practice of relaxation training should be made, and the client should not be overconfident about being able to maintain the skill without practicing.

GUIDELINES FOR DETERMINING A TRAINING TIMETABLE

There is really only one rule to follow in determining the rate at which the therapist trains the client in the more efficient relaxation procedures outlined in this chapter: never introduce a new procedure until the client has mastered the previous one. This rule is deceptively simple, however, since it is often difficult to determine just when the client is ready to move on to the next step in training. Before suggesting how the therapist might obtain this information, we would like to present a relatively conservative timetable for progress. This timetable is conservative in that most clients proceed more rapidly than is indicated in the schedule presented below. However, it is ultimately less disruptive to move too slowly than to "push" a client through the procedures. Any overlearning which may occur if the therapist follows the timetable presented here will probably be beneficial to the client in the long run.

We suggest that the initial procedure (utilizing sixteen muscle groups) be employed for at least the first three sessions. If the client is being seen once a week, this would allow for two full weeks of practice and for two sessions with the therapist during which any problems arising at home might be discussed. The importance of the client's mastery of these initial techniques cannot be overemphasized. Therefore, three sessions of the sixteen-group procedure does not seem unreasonable. If at the fourth session the client is achieving satisfactory relaxation without difficulty (according to the rules which we will outline below), the seven-group procedure should be introduced. The new procedure should be practiced by the client during the next week and employed again at the next session in order to insure that it is being used correctly and to the client's satisfaction. The four-group procedure may be instituted at the sixth session and continued into the seventh. The recall procedure would be introduced at the eighth session, and repeated at the ninth (perhaps with the counting procedure added, depending upon the client's reports). Counting alone may then be employed at session ten and at all subsequent sessions.

If all goes according to plan, the relaxation timetable would be as follows:

Procedure	Session
16 muscle groups, tension-release	1,2,3
7 muscle groups, tension-release	4,5
4 muscle groups, tension-release	6,7
4 muscle groups, recall	8
4 muscle groups, recall and counting	9
Counting	10

Note that, except for introducing counting at the end of session 9, the therapist conducts each new procedure at least twice before moving on to the next step.

Again, we would like to emphasize that this schedule, which suggests that the client start learning the counting procedure by the tenth session, is only a theoretical outline. The important concern is that of client skill and satisfaction at each step in the training program. Resolution of these issues is the main prerequisite for proceeding to the next step.

Many clients will want to please the therapist and attempt to hide difficulties that have occurred in practice sessions; therefore, the therapist must be constantly alert for indications of troubles which are not reported by the client. Perhaps the main indirect signal of the presence of problems is the client's failure to fulfill practice obligations. The client should, and indeed must, practice the assigned procedures as directed; if this is not occurring, it may mean that the relaxation experience is insufficiently reinforcing to maintain regular efforts at improving it. (This point, as well as others related to problems with practice assignments, is considered in Chapter 9.) Deviations from the "two-a-day" routine (with the exception of minor inconsistencies caused by unexpected events) normally warrant delay in moving through the training program. For example, if a client reports having practiced the procedures as prescribed two or three days out of seven, the therapist should probably not proceed to the next step in training until the client is practicing on a regular basis. It is inadvisable to mention this to the client, lest he/she give false reports in impatience to make progress. Rather, gentle but firm insistence on consistent practice should suffice.

Related to practice regularity is the client's continuity of progress. Clients who report encountering no major difficulties in relaxation but fail to show progress in terms of increased speed, efficiency, and degree of comfort may be withholding information. (Some suggestions for assessing clients' progress in relaxation training are presented in Chapter 10.)

8 Differential and Conditioned Relaxation

DIFFERENTIAL RELAXATION

Differential relaxation is one of the most common applications of the basic progressive relaxation skill. As Jacobson has pointed out, a variety of muscles become tensed during most behaviors. Muscles necessary for the accomplishment of an activity are frequently more tense than they need to be, and muscles unnecessary for efficient performance become tense during the activity. In both cases, there is residual tension which contributes nothing to the behavior and which needlessly increases psychological stress. Ideally, in terms of conservation of energy and maintenance of a low tension level, *only* those muscles directly relevant to an activity should be tense *only* to the degree required for efficient performance of the activity.

Differential relaxation can help clients to approach this ideal situation. Deep relaxation is induced and maintained in the muscles not required for the ongoing activity. For muscles involved in the activity, excess tension is eliminated; only the amount of tension necessary for behavioral performance remains. The result is that the client can perform most daily activities with a minimum of tension and a maximum of relaxed comfort.

Proper and consistent use of differential relaxation has three advantages. First, for any individual involved in progressive relaxation training, it provides many opportunities to practice, and thus improve, the skill of relaxation. Second, for chronically tense individuals, it helps maintain lowered arousal throughout the day. Third, for individuals who become tense only in particular situations, it allows for situation-specific relaxation.

The procedure essentially involves the periodic identification of tension during daily activities and the subsequent relaxation of muscles that are unnecessarily tense. Identification of tension is, of course, one of the skills that are learned during progressive relaxation train-ing. Relaxation of those muscles identified as tense may then be accomplished by using either tension-release cycles or recall. (The method used depends on the stage of relaxation training the client has reached at the time differential relaxation is introduced.)

Practice Procedures

The suggested program for differential relaxation involves a series of practice steps beginning with relatively quiet activities and continuing with more active behaviors. In quiet activities, nonessential muscles predominate, and practice is similar to basic relaxation. As the client continues with more complex behaviors, tension identification and elimination become quite easy.

There are three continua over which the practice may develop. Lower levels of each continuum involve less distractions and the client may more easily concentrate on the relaxation process. The three continua are situation, position, and activity level. Situation varies from being alone in a quiet room to being with others in a noisy place. Position varies from sitting to standing. Activity level ranges from inactivity to routine complex movements.

The client should first practice defining essential and nonessential muscle groups for various activities. It is important that the client not only become aware of the necessary muscle groups involved but can also identify and be sensitive to the nonessential ones. Simply discuss various daily activities in terms of the muscle groups required for their performance.

The second task is to assign "homework" for practicing differential relaxation. The scheduling of such practice can follow eight steps combining the continua values. These steps, along with a typical example of each, are presented below:

1. Sitting, nonactive, quiet place: e.g. sitting upright in

a chair in a bedroom

2. Sitting, nonactive, nonquiet place: e.g. sitting in a cafeteria
3. Sitting, active, quiet place: e.g. typing in a study
4. Sitting, active, nonquiet place: e.g. eating in a cafeteria
5. Standing, nonactive, quiet place: e.g. standing in a living room
6. Standing, nonactive, nonquiet place: e.g. waiting in a ticket line
7. Standing, active, quiet place: e.g. working alone at a counter
8. Standing, active, nonquiet place: e.g. walking outside

The first step involves a transition from the usual relaxation practice position (all muscles supported, eyes closed) to a common sitting posture (head supported by neck muscles, eyes open). The client is instructed to periodically relax all muscle groups by using either tension-release cycles or recall. There will be residual tension remaining in eye and neck muscles, but this tension is to be minimal. All other muscles are to be relaxed.

Steps 2 through 8 involve increasing distraction as well as activity in more muscle groups. The procedure is the same: first identify, then eliminate, the tension in each nonessential muscle group. There is no need to be concerned about residual tension in muscles required for performance of ongoing behavior.

Progress in this Technique

The progress of the client through these eight steps should be determined by his/her ability to relax non-essential muscles deeply and to relax essential muscles to the point where tension in them is not uncomfortable. Once this goal is consistently achieved at one step, the client may continue to the next step, proceeding at his/her own rate. The speed of progress is, of course, dependent upon the frequency and quality of practice. A reasonable timetable would be the following: first week—step 1; second week—steps 2, 3, and 4; third week—steps 5, 6, 7, and 8.

This timetable assumes that the client is at least at the four muscle group stage of basic relaxation training and that he/she practices each differential relaxation step for no more than 5 minutes four times a day. Once the client is able to relax fairly well in step 8 conditions, the therapist should encourage frequent relaxations throughout the day. The ultimate goal can be characterized by the following example.

A client is driving to work. He needs to use the muscles of his eyes, neck, arms, hands, right foot, and leg. After starting the motor, he identifies tension and relaxes in each of the four muscle groups, all in about 60 seconds. As he is driving, he may periodically notice tension in unused muscles or discomfort in used muscles. This may be quickly eliminated by recall. He parks his car and walks a few blocks to his place of work. As he is walking he relaxes some tension in his facial and trunk muscles. At his desk, he gets comfortably seated and spends a few seconds eliminating tension in all muscles. He repeats this each time he sits down. Further, while doing paper work, if he notices uncomfortable tension in his writing arm, he spends a moment relaxing it by recall.

The client should know two things about this procedure. First, it is not intended that nonessential muscles be completely inactive. The idea is to limit activity to a minimum but not to such an extent that ongoing behavior is disrupted. Second, although it initially takes some deliberate effort to remember to use differential relaxation procedures, as the skill increases and becomes habitual, very little time and effort are required.

CONDITIONED RELAXATION

The goal of *conditioned relaxation* training is to enable the client to achieve relaxation in response to a self-produced cue. Paul (1966) described the procedure as follows:

> "After the client is totally relaxed, he is instructed to focus all of his attention on his own breathing, and then to subvocalize a cue word each time he exhales—such as "calm," "relax," etc. . . . The therapist repeats the word in synchrony with exhalation 5 times, and the client then continues for 15 more pairings. After repeating this procedure over a period of 4 or 5 weeks, with the client giving 20 additional pairings on his own each night following relaxation practice, the ability of the self-produced cue word to bring about relaxation may be tested in the office. This is done by having the client image a threatening situation until some degree of anxiety is experienced, then he is instructed to take a deep breath, and subvocalize the cue word on exhalation. If a relaxation response is achieved, the client may be instructed to use this cue anytime he begins to feel a slight inappropriate increase in anxiety in any real-life situation."*

In conditioned relaxation, the client is first trained in progressive relaxation and then taught an association between the resulting deeply relaxed state and a self-produced cue word such as "calm," "control" or "relax." Once the client has learned to use such cues to produce relaxation, he/she can reduce tension in day-to-day stress situations. For many clients, skill in conditioned relaxation results in a reduction both in general tension and in anxiety prior to a stressful event. The client feels less helpless when confronted by daily problems and transient stress. Many clients report feeling less anxious about "things in general" because they know they have an effective means of controlling the tension produced by difficult life situations.

A Case Study

An example of the use of conditioned relaxation techniques as part of a more general therapeutic intervention is provided by a colleague.* The client was a female college student in her junior year who sought help because of difficulties in relating to men, concerns about moral standards, and problems of stress due to academic and social overcommitment. During the third session, she reported that she sometimes became "choked" during periods of strong stress. The problem had become so acute that, on at least one occasion, she was gasping for breath and was hospitalized. Tranquilizers had been prescribed for the problem but could not prevent what was clearly a tension-produced hyperventilation problem.

The client was trained in progressive relaxation and after a few sessions was asked to subvocalize the words "calm, control" on exhaling while deeply relaxed. This procedure was repeated at each relaxation session and the client was asked to repeat the procedure at each home practice session. At the same time, the therapist helped the client to assess various stress-producing aspects of her life, and the number of realistic external sources of anxiety was reduced. Taking steps to reduce the number of stressful elements in the client's life while directing conditioned relaxation training was extremely effective in this case. Over the four-month period of therapy, the client reported being much more comfortable, both because of fewer external problems and because of an increased ability to control tension in unavoidable stress situations (such as final examinations).

CONDITIONED VERSUS DIFFERENTIAL RELAXATION

Conditioned relaxation can be taught instead of or in

*Paul, G. L. Insight vs. Desensitization in Psychotherapy. Stanford: Stanford University Press, 1966.

*The authors wish to thank Dr. Lester Tobias for making this case report available.

addition to differential relaxation, depending upon the time available and the therapist's goals. Differential relaxation is obviously the more specific, since it involves reduction of tension in certain muscle groups which are unnecessary for a given activity. This results in the maintenance of a comfortable state of arousal in any situation, stressful or not. Conditioned relaxation, on the other hand, is a more generalized skill which is best employed in producing nonspecific tension reduction in the face of stress.

9 Possible Problems—
Suggested Solutions

In most cases, relaxation training procedures do not run as smoothly as does the recorded illustration which accompanies this manual, nor does progress through the various steps of training always occur without setbacks and problems. A wide variety of difficulties can occur in all phases of training: in any session, from the first to the last, or during the client's home practice. The particular set of problems the therapist is likely to encounter is never constant; it varies radically from client to client and even from one point in training to another. Thus, a client who had little or no difficulty in learning the initial techniques may later experience great difficulty, while another client may take many weeks to master the basic sixteen-groups procedure and then progress rapidly through the remaining procedures.

It is difficult, if not impossible, to predict the kinds of problems which will occur in any given case, and perhaps the best way to avoid major trouble is to carefully study this manual and to strictly adhere to the more important rules presented in it. In addition, the therapist should pay careful attention to seemingly inconsequential difficulties occurring early in training since they may have disastrous consequences at some later point. Small errors should be corrected at an early date to avoid allowing the client to practice incorrect procedures. Such practice would make it very difficult for the client to later master the appropriate techniques.

As an example, the therapist may have a client who has difficulty in keeping attention focused on the feelings of relaxation. If this situation is not corrected through the use of indirect suggestion and other focusing techniques, training in relaxation by recall may be extremely difficult. At this point the therapist would have to retrain a client who has learned to allow his/her attention to wander during relaxation practice.

The therapist should always be alert for trouble occurring anywhere in relaxation training, but must also learn to recognize the difference between important problems and those which are in fact trivial. This is not always easy. The therapist should decide whether or not the difficulty or the deviation from standard procedure is likely to either decrease the probability of relaxation in an office session or in home practice or cause a client to fail to achieve skill in an area which will be necessary later. (For example, practicing relaxation in a noisy, disruptive setting would decrease the probability of relaxation; and failing to insure that the client is attending to feelings in the muscles would make later mastery of relaxation by recall difficult, if not impossible.) If the problem reported by the client or the deviation from standard procedure meets either of these criteria, then the therapist should eliminate the problem and/or return as closely as possible to standard procedure.

If, on the other hand, the difficulty or deviation meets neither of these criteria, the therapist should do no more than simply "keep an eye on it" so that no undesirable consequences result. As an example of an inconsequential problem we might cite the use of a unique alternative tensing strategy which succeeds in producing the desired tension. In this case the important thing is to achieve tension in the muscle group even at the expense of abandoning standard procedure. Thus, deviation from standard procedure is to be desired when the client would not benefit from adherence to standard procedure. Another example might involve a client who finds it difficult or impossible to relax if the chair is fully reclined. While standard procedure calls for the client to be in the fully reclined position, it is the client's comfort which is of primary concern, and the therapist can allow the relaxation sessions to occur in a semi-reclined or even an upright position if this facilitates the proceedings. As a final example, we might encounter a client who desires not to remove a ring, wristwatch, or even eyeglasses. The probability of such a deviation seriously interfering with attainment of deep relaxation is low, and the therapist need not insist on compliance with standard rules.

As problems arise in the course of training, the therapist must make responsible decisions. Will the problem seriously affect the course of relaxation training? Is its resolution vital to the success of the program? If the problem is potentially disruptive, the therapist must take steps to resolve it. If, on the other hand, the therapist believes the problem to be trivial, he/she can treat it in a relaxed "let's not worry about it" manner.

Above all, no client should ever be made to feel that he/she has a special problem the therapist has never faced before and which may not have a solution. If the therapist believes the problem to be trivial, the client should also understand this and not become overly concerned. If, on the other hand, the therapist feels that the issue needs to be resolved, this should be done in a manner designed to keep the client's anxiety about the problem low and confidence in the therapist high. Even in the case of a problem for which there is no ready solution, the therapist should not take the approach that this is a completely unique difficulty which will ultimately destroy the client's chances of learning relaxation skills. The client should for one week carefully observe the status of the trouble during practice sessions. The therapist can use this week to devise a solution to this particular difficulty and, in many cases, the week of practice eliminates the problem. The important concern is that the client be as comfortable as possible throughout the relaxation training. He/she should be reinforced for any progress made and not made to feel inadequate or incompetent at the appearance of problems.

In the sections to follow we have made a list of some of the most common problems, along with some helpful solution techniques.

MUSCLE CRAMPS

The occurrence of muscle cramps during relaxation training is very disruptive and should be avoided. Cramps occur most frequently in the calves and feet. Cramps can be avoided by asking the client to generate less tension in these problem areas for a shorter period of time (no longer than 5 seconds for the feet).

If cramps do occur, they are likely to disrupt a state of relaxation, and the client may sit up and manipulate the cramped muscles. The therapist should, however, encourage the client to stay in the reclined position with eyes closed and simply move the cramped muscles while allowing other muscles in the body to remain at rest. After the cramp is relieved and the client reports no discomfort, the therapist should, for at least one minute, provide indirect suggestions about returning to the previous state of relaxation and then continue with the standard procedure, using a 3-5 second tension cycle with the group which had cramped.

If, with a particular client, cramping occurs in the same muscle group every time it is tensed, the therapist will have to implement an alternative tensing strategy; the client and the therapist should work together to find alternative procedures.

MOVEMENT

Even though the client has been instructed not to move a muscle group unnecessarily once it has been relaxed, the therapist may observe a considerable amount of movement during a relaxation training session. This may take the form of "fidgeting" to find a more comfortable position in the chair; it may involve scratching various parts of the body such as the ears or nose; it may involve "stretching" different parts of the body such as the hands or feet. Such movement can usually be ignored, especially if the therapist feels that the client is trying to get more comfortable or relieve some momentary discomfort such as an itch. Such movements are not likely to seriously disrupt the progress of training.

However, frequent and widespread movement which occurs during virtually the entire training session (for more than one session) is a serious problem, mainly because it indicates that the client is not relaxing. The therapist should consider the possibility that the relaxation training is not being adequately directed. The trouble may be a failure to properly communicate instructions; the therapist should remind the client not to move muscle groups unnecessarily once they have been relaxed. In many cases a reiteration of instructions will be an effective solution. If, however, movement of large muscle groups continues, the therapist should improve the presentation of relaxation instructions since it is obviously not producing the desired results.

The therapist's goal is not a client with a corpse-like appearance; rather the client should resemble a sleeper, moving only slightly and occasionally.

LAUGHTER OR TALKING

Early in training especially (primarily during the first session), some clients may find the training procedures humorous and begin laughing. The best response to this behavior is to simply ignore it. This means not responding to the laughter in any way, treating it as if it were not occurring. If this tactic is consistently employed, the therapist can be certain that the inappropriate behavior will be eliminated, unless the therapist is behaving in a way which is directly causing the client to laugh (e.g. sounding very theatrical in the presentation of the relaxation instructions). If the therapist believes that his/her own behavior, rather than the initiation of a new and unfamiliar activity, is causing the laughter, this should be resolved during the questioning which immediately follows the first training session.

Since the client was instructed to communicate with the therapist only through hand signals, any verbal behavior displayed by the client should be discouraged. One class of such behavior can be eliminated by *extinction*, that is, by ignoring it. These behaviors are most likely to occur early in the first session and are usually attempts to respond to the therapist's instructions. For example, the therapist might say, "O.K., now I'd like you to focus all of your attention on the muscles of your right hand and lower arm." The client might then say, "O.K., I'm doing that." If such behavior receives no response, the client, especially as greater relaxation is achieved, will usually stop emitting the behavior without any specific instructions from the therapist.

If extinction does not eliminate the client's verbal behavior by the end of the first session, the therapist should simply reiterate the relevant instructions to the client. This might be done as early as halfway through the first session when an especially verbose client is disrupting presentation of the relaxation instructions.

The most important verbal behaviors which can be emitted by a client during a session are reports of a serious problem which requires immediate therapist attention. An example of this might be a report of some extreme discomfort; verbal behaviors of this type should not be ignored.

Thus, except in the case of statements by the client which indicate a serious problem, most talking and laughing can be eliminated through either extinction or the reiteration of instructions.

EXTERNAL NOISE

Ideally, relaxation training should take place in a sound-proof room. This is almost never possible, however, and it is likely that some noise from outside the consulting room will be intruding. The client is going to be stimulated by auditory input sources such as typewriters, telephones, airplanes, or, as in one case in the authors' experience, even a jackhammer. The therapist should take all possible steps to minimize such external noise. If a typist can be requested to cease his/her activity for an hour or so, or if nearby telephones can be disconnected or turned down, this should be done. While the ideal of a completely quiet room should be as closely approximated as possible, in many cases there is nothing that a therapist can do about noise. But rather than be discouraged by the situation, the therapist should simply proceed as if the noise did not exist. Of course, if it is impossible for the therapist to make himself heard over the interference, a new location should be sought. In most cases, as long as the client can hear the therapist, even loud outside noise will not have an ultimately destructive effect on the progress of relaxation training. Indeed, the presence of such noise will increase the client's relaxation skill in home practice sessions since the probability that the client's home environment includes a completely quiet room is low. If the client can learn the skills under less than ideal conditions, he/she can certainly practice them under such conditions. In addition, if the skills are to be applied in real-life situations, the presence of real-life noise during the learning process would be helpful in terms of generalization of applicability.

SPASMS AND TICS

Especially in clients who are initially very tense and who have not had much experience with deep relaxation, the therapist may note the presence of muscle spasms during relaxation training. These may be described by the client as "twitching," "tics," or "jerking." They are muscle spasms which are correlated with muscle relaxation and occur in many people when they fall asleep. Their occurrence during a session, however, may be disconcerting to the client, and, while they do not constitute a major problem, it is important that the therapist respond well in the situation. If the spasms do not seem to be disrupting the progress of relaxation, any comments on the issue may be made after the session is over; otherwise, the therapist should state that spasms should not be a matter of concern, that they simply indicate that relaxation is going well, and that the client should neither worry about nor try to prevent them. The client and therapist can discuss this in more detail after the session. The therapist can mention that spasms are very common and often occur prior to sleep. He/she should also point out that such spasms are noticeable during a session because the client is awake, focusing on his/her muscles, and probably not used to experiencing deep relaxation in a waking state.

INTRUSIVE THOUGHTS

Perhaps the most disruptive factor the client can present is the presence of distracting, intrusive thoughts. During a relaxation session the client may become anxious or aroused as a result of various thoughts which occur to him/her. The client may begin focusing on these thoughts rather than continue giving full attention to feelings of tension and relaxation.

This class of problems must be dealt with effectively if the therapist is to succeed in training the client in relaxation skills. The presence of intrusive thinking will probably become evident to the therapist early in training, and the time to deal with it is at the conclusion of the first session in which they occur. Note that we are dealing specifically with intrusive thoughts, not just any thoughts. Thoughts which are not incompatible with relaxation need not be eliminated; the client does not need a "blank mind" in order for relaxation training to be successful.

Anxiety-Producing Thoughts

There are two major classes of intrusive thoughts. The first of these includes those thoughts which result in anxiety, fear, or discomfort for the client simply because they are occurring. These thoughts may relate to the reason the client sought professional help, or they may relate to other sources. The client may focus on financial difficulties, crises in the home situation, suicide, or on any of a wide variety of other upsetting things. Unfortunately it is usually not sufficient to simply tell the client to "stop thinking about those things." Some alternative technique for keeping the client's attention focused upon the task at hand is required. We have in the past found the use of two interrelated procedures to be helpful.

The first is to increase the amount of talking on the therapist's part, keeping the client listening to and focusing on the instructions, without even a 5- or 10-second silence during which thoughts might begin to wander. The therapist should couple the increased patter with reiterated instructions to the client to remain focused on the instructions. While this tactic is usually helpful in keeping the client from "wandering off" during the office sessions, it usually cannot maintain the client's focused attention during practice sessions at home. Therefore, some additional procedures are helpful.

The best means of helping a client avoid the disruptive effects of anxiety-producing thoughts is to determine an alternative set of thoughts upon which to focus. Feelings of relaxation are often not sufficiently clear to provide a consistent focal point for the client. The client and therapist should confer and specify a set of neutral or pleasant images to focus on during home practice or even during office sessions. The therapist should ask for a description of a time when the client was very relaxed and happy, perhaps a vacation or a time from his/her childhood. Specific content does not matter, as long as this was a pleasant (or at least neutral) setting and time which the client enjoys thinking about. The time, the situation, and the setting should be discussed in detail so that the therapist can describe it clearly and thus help the client focus on these images.

If possible, the therapist should try to extract from this "pleasant image" some rather monotonous relaxing factors to add to the "patter." If the pleasant image involves lying on a beach on a summer day, the therapist would want to take advantage of the fact that waves strike the beach in a rhythmic way and mention that the client can "almost hear the sound of the water lapping against the shore." The therapist should integrate some aspect of the image into the relaxation "patter" so that relaxation and the image become part of one another; the therapist does not want the client to be focusing on the pleasant image and excluding the ongoing process of relaxation. Ideally, the client who has trouble with anxiety-producing intrusive thoughts should be provided with some pleasant scenes to visualize. These scenes should be easily integrated into the relaxation procedure and act to facilitate it.

Sexual Arousal

The second major category of intrusive thoughts involves the problem of sexual arousal on the part of the client during relaxation sessions. It must be recognized that, especially when the therapist and client are not members of the same sex, there are many possibly seductive aspects to the procedure. The therapist and client are together in a dimly lit room, the client is in a recumbent or semi-recumbent position, and the therapist is speaking softly while suggesting very pleasant images and feelings.

The therapist should not become overly concerned if the client evidences some sexual arousal during a session. Rather it should be regarded as just another type of intrusive thinking which interferes with relaxation training. As such, it is a subject for discussion during post-questioning. Of course, if the arousal and the anxiety it may produce for the client are of such a magnitude that the client's concentration is disrupted, the therapist would be wise to interrupt the session to discuss the relevant issues immediately. Whether the problem occurs with a member of the opposite sex or with a member of the same sex (in the case of "homosexual panic" during a session), it is best to suggest that the client's reaction to the situation is not at all unusual. The therapist can even name the aspects of the situation which are seductive, just as they are listed here. It should be emphasized, however, that as the client practices at home, he/she will learn to focus on the new skill itself rather than on the therapist's presentation technique. The client should be reassured that this is not an uncommon or major difficulty and that there is no cause for anxiety. (If as time goes by, however, it becomes clear that a "real" sexual attachment is being formed, then the therapist will want to take whatever steps he/she sees necessary in this clinical situation.) The therapist should remember that sexual arousal may often develop, early in training especially, and that if it is treated relatively casually by the therapist, it will not become a major source of disruption.

SLEEP

One of the most common, and certainly most annoying, problems which can arise in the course of progressive relaxation training is having the client fall asleep during a training session. This certainly indicates that the therapist is not doing anything which is keeping the client upset or aroused, but it must be avoided if relaxation skills are to be learned efficiently. First the therapist must determine if and when the client is asleep, then devise techniques for keeping the client awake in subsequent sessions.

Determining that a subject is asleep is not always as easy as it might seem. It is sometimes difficult to discriminate a sleeping client from one who is signaling incomplete relaxation. For example, the therapist may ask the client for a signal if the muscles in the abdominal region are completely relaxed; if there is no signal, the therapist can direct another tension-release cycle in this area and determine from the response, or lack of it, whether or not the client is asleep. This is the procedure to use when training is in the observable tensing and relaxing phase. A good alternative procedure for later phases of relaxation training is to ask for a *double confirmation of consciousness*. The therapist should ask for a signal if the muscles in question feel completely relaxed. If there is no signal, and the therapist suspects that the client may be asleep, he/she can then ask for a signal if the muscle group in question is *not* completely relaxed. Unless the client is asleep, the therapist will receive a response to one of these two questions. This simple technique can save the unwitting therapist from continuing to repeat recall cycles with a sleeping client.

The double confirmation procedure should be used frequently where the client tends to go to sleep easily, and only occasionally with other clients. However, at the recall phase it should be used at least part of the time for all clients.

If the therapist ascertains that the client is asleep, he/she should continue to speak in a progressively louder voice until the client responds. These continued suggestions or requests can be spaced at 10-15 second intervals, and the therapist should be careful not to startle the client and disrupt the state of relaxation that has been achieved.

A client who reports falling asleep regularly when practicing at home should be encouraged to attempt to remain awake until the entire practice procedure has been completed.

The following are a few techniques for avoiding sleep during relaxation training (that is, on the part of the client; the problem of the therapist falling asleep has not as yet been fully researched).

The therapist should instruct the client to sleep for at least eight hours on the nights before relaxation training sessions. While this may be difficult for some clients, the goal should be approximated as closely as possible. The therapist should also avoid scheduling training sessions very early in the morning or immediately after the noon meal.

The therapist should also determine whether to begin speaking louder and less monotonously. After listening to tape recordings of the sessions and asking the client's opinion, the therapist can decide how much to adjust voice volume and tone. But there should be no need to shout to keep the client awake; making only slight changes in voice quality usually suffices.

For more extreme cases, the client should be given direct instructions to focus on the sound of the therapist's voice while keeping the muscles of the body deeply relaxed. These instructions should be integrated into the relaxation "patter," not just given before the session. Thus, the therapist should interject into the "patter" such statements as the following: "Noticing now that as these muscles become more and more deeply and completely relaxed, you're able to focus very clearly and alertly on the sound of my voice," or "Focusing all of your attention now on the sound of my voice and the sound of your smooth and regular breathing as the muscles become more and more deeply relaxed."

Should these procedures fail to eliminate the sleep problem, the relaxation intervals should be reduced to a maximum of 30 seconds so that the client does not have as long a time to focus on relaxation. The therapist should be very careful to strike a balance between keeping relaxation depth above the level which produces sleep and keeping it below the point at which it is not different from the normal waking state. Drastic reduction of relaxation intervals is not recommended except in the most extreme cases and after other techniques designed to avoid sleep have been given a fair trial (including sufficient home practice).

COUGHING AND SNEEZING

We have already discussed some client behavior interruptions such as talking, falling asleep, and having muscle spasms; two other disrupting client behaviors are coughing and sneezing. These are not usually major problems and, especially when a client is in good health and the coughing or sneezing occurs only once or twice during a session, it can usually be ignored. The therapist may take notice of these interruptions only to provide brief reassurance to the client that coughs and sneezes should not interfere with relaxing. The client should also be told to cough or sneeze again if necessary since attempting to inhibit the behavior results in an increase in muscle tension.

If disruptive coughing and sneezing is the result of an illness, the therapist should decide whether the session should be postponed until the client has regained his/her health. A client with a severe head cold may have neither the ability nor the inclination to remain motionless and ignore discomfort long enough to achieve relaxation. If it seems that the session will lose all effectiveness through continued interruptions, it should be postponed.

Perhaps a more frustrating problem is the smoker's cough, which is likely to cause trouble whenever the client is asked to take a deep breath and hold it. Many heavy or even moderate smokers will find it difficult to refrain from coughing when taking a deep breath. In such cases, the client should take a breath while tensing, but not inhale quite so deeply. Another alternative procedure involves asking the client to exhale (not too vigorously) while these muscles are tensed and to then resume normal breathing as the muscles are released. Should both shallower inhalations and the exhalation procedure fail to eliminate the problem, the therapist would have to eliminate the breath-holding technique from the procedures. The client should, of course, be given some time to practice the alternative procedures before the therapist abandons them as useless.

INABILITY TO RELAX SPECIFIC MUSCLE GROUPS

Often a client will report continuing difficulty in relaxing specific muscle groups. This may occur even in cases where the therapist and client have determined an alternative tensing strategy (as outlined in Chapter 5). The alternative strategy may work only temporarily and if a client reports again experiencing difficulty, the therapist should immediately find a new procedure. If a variety of alternative strategies have been employed without success, the therapist can begin to suspect that the problem is due to the presence of intrusive thoughts (see section on intrusive thoughts). In most cases, however, the inability to achieve relaxation in particular muscle groups will disappear with regular practice of alternative tensing procedures.

Some clients may feel that the standard relaxation procedure does not produce complete relaxation because a relevant muscle group (e.g. the muscles of the lower back) has been neglected. The therapist and client should work together to develop a tensing strategy for those muscles (e.g. having the client lift himself/herself very slightly out of the chair using the lower back muscles). Thus, in cases of residual tension in a muscle group not included in the standard procedure, the therapist should simply develop a new tensing strategy, not ignore the problem area because it is not mentioned as part of the procedure outlined in Chapters 5, 6, and 7.

STRANGE OR UNFAMILIAR FEELINGS DURING RELAXATION

Many of the sensations associated with deep relaxation seem to produce unusual sensations in the body because the client has either never before focused on feelings of relaxation or has never before been deeply relaxed. The reported feelings often involve lack of orientation in space: the client may feel he/she is floating and may not be able to determine the position of his/her arms and legs in relation to the rest of the body. Such general disorientation is often accompanied by feelings of warmth, tingling, coolness, etc. On occasion these feelings can become frightening to the client, and the therapist must respond reassuringly.

First, the therapist should mention that these feelings are commonly experienced when learning relaxation techniques and that they provide evidence that the client is acquiring the skills successfully. The client should be encouraged to enjoy, rather than fear, the sensations associated with deep relaxation. If these instructions fail to provide adequate reassurance, the therapist can ask the client to open his/her eyes and, without moving, simply look around the room and at his/her own body, then continue relaxation with eyes closed. The client should be told to perform this reorientation activity at any time, either in the office or at home, whenever strange feelings cause anxiety. The client should not fear new sensations, but realize what they are and learn to eliminate any anxiety they cause.

"LOSING CONTROL" DURING RELAXATION

Occasionally, the systematic tensing and release of various muscle groups and focusing attention on consequent sensations (all of which are necessary for the success of relaxation training) are themselves part of the client's problem. This presents a serious difficulty for the therapist and occurs most frequently in clients who "lose control" of their behaviors or emotional states. In these cases, routine employment of the standard relaxation procedures is ill-advised. The subjective experiences involved in relaxation may seem very strange and, unless these feelings are interpreted as pleasant controllable experiences, the client may feel even less "in control."

In our experience have been two cases of this type. The first client's problem involved fears of tensing his muscles! In the past, deliberately tensing his muscles had resulted in feelings of dissociation, loss of control, and flashback scenes of early childhood fears. The second client complained of "losing control" and "going crazy" whenever he was alone or began staring at an object. Standard relaxation procedures would have required the client to perform behaviors (tensing and attention-focusing) which historically were stimuli for anxiety.

Problems of this nature are easily resolved by adding three special steps to the basic training procedure. First, even more attention must be given to discussing the subjective experiences that the client is likely to notice during therapy. It must be stressed that it is the client himself, not the therapist, who is producing these experiences and that though they may be somewhat new, they will be very pleasant.

Secondly, introduction of the basic procedures should be more gradual. The first session may include no more than an extended version of the demonstration session which typically precedes actual relaxation training. That is, the client may sit in a regular chair with eyes open, and the lights should be left on. The therapist should then model the tension-release cycles of the various muscle groups while the client imitates the procedures and reports on any subjective sensations as they occur. Attention should be repeatedly drawn to the fact that the client can control tension and relaxation and the feelings they produce. The therapist should help the client identify and label the feelings which occur during the session. The therapist's instructions should remain conversational in tone. Homework assignments should be patterned after this session: lights on, sitting upright, eyes open.

As the client progresses, conditions may be made increasingly similar to the standard training procedure. Recommended changes, in progressive order, are (1) having the client recline, (2) turning off the lights, and (3) having the client close his/her eyes. The therapist's voice should gradually become less conversational and begin to approximate the more monotonous tone illustrated on the record which accompanies this manual.

Finally, during post-questioning, more attention should be directed toward insuring that the positive expectancies established earlier are being fulfilled. The client should describe any novel sensations and be assured that these feelings are commonly reported consequences of deep muscular relaxation. It is wise to remind the client that the goal of relaxation skill training is to *increase* the client's *control* over subjective emotional states.

"INTERNAL AROUSAL"

Occasionally clients will report that at the end of a

relaxation training session they have no tension in the muscle groups, but that they feel "tight" or tense "inside." They may feel tense or even anxious internally while experiencing deep relaxation peripherally. The therapist should explain to the client that the internal tension involves muscles which are not under voluntary control and that the relaxation training procedure directly affects muscles under voluntary control. The therapist should also point out that these voluntary and involuntary systems are interrelated and that, with practice, "shutdown" of the peripheral muscles will eventually produce relaxation at the internal level.

Again note that the client should not become upset about the problem, or feel that he/she is unusual or strange. Relaxation will generalize from the peripheral voluntary groups included in relaxation training to the central nonvoluntary groups which had remained somewhat aroused. As the client's ability to deeply relax voluntary muscles increases, heart rate, respiration, and other internal processes "shut down" in like manner.

If such resolution of the problem fails to occur, the therapist can be sure that the client has not been adequately trained in the relaxation procedures themselves. The therapist should closely examine the presentation of training procedures to assure that relaxation in all muscle groups, and especially in those directly adjacent to the arousal (the muscles of the chest, the back, and the abdomen), is being achieved.

FAILURE TO FOLLOW INSTRUCTIONS

It may happen that the client does not correctly follow instructions. This is especially likely to occur early in training. There are two main reasons for such failure to comply with instructions: either the client has forgotten or misinterpreted the instructions, or he/she is attempting to control the situation by behaving independently of them. Because there are many instructions and they often seem complicated, it is probably better to assume that the client has simply failed to understand or interpret correctly the instructions as given. The instruction which is not being carried out appropriately

should therefore be repeated.

For example, the client may be tensing a muscle group prior to the "now" signal, thereby making it difficult for the therapist to accurately time tension cycles. The client may be releasing tension gradually or independently initiating his/her own tension cycles while the therapist is giving relaxation instructions. The therapist should simply remind the client of the standard procedure by saying, for example, "O.K., that was fine. Now remember, next time do not begin tensing the muscle groups until I give you the signal 'now'," or "O.K., you're doing fine, just remember to release all the tension at once rather than letting it go gradually," or "Remember to tense muscle groups only on my instruction. Stay focused in on the sound of my voice and try as best you can to do the things I tell you to do." The therapist is in the role of the teacher reminding a student of the procedures to be followed. The therapist should *not* assume a punitive attitude.

If the client is attempting to gain control of the situation, the therapist response should be identical to that outlined in the previous paragraph: the therapist should simply continue to reissue the same instructions so the client does not "get away with" independent action. Thus, if instructions to tense only on cue have been given twice and the client is still tensing independently, the therapist should continue repeating the tension cycle on the same muscle group until the client tenses on cue. Whether failure to follow instructions is an innocent error or not, the therapist must maintain control of the situation and not allow the session to proceed when the client is being uncooperative. If the therapist feels that lack of cooperativeness is a problem area in relation to other concerns which brought the client to the therapist, it should be discussed, usually after the relaxation session is concluded. If the problem is such that the session cannot continue until it is resolved, the procedures may have to be terminated until the resolution is reached.

PROBLEMS WITH PRACTICING

When the client fails to practice assignments at home,

this is also a problem of failure to follow instructions, but because this particular failure occurs outside of the sessions, we are considering it separately.

There are two major reasons why clients do not practice as instructed. The first involves features of the physical environment or daily schedule which make it difficult for the client to accomplish, or to remember to accomplish, the practice assignments. The second class of reasons is more serious; the relaxation procedures themselves may be unrewarding to the client because they are not producing the reduction in arousal which is the goal of the training.

Whatever the reason for failure to practice, there is one aspect of therapist behavior which should remain constant. This is emphasis to the client of the importance of practice. The therapist can use a physical conditioning analogy, a "learning to read" analogy, or any other, but it must be clear to the client that the skill will not develop unless practice occurs regularly.

Where there are some modifiable factors in the environment preventing adequate practice, the therapist and client need to work out more suitable arrangements. This may mean changing the time of practice or the physical setting, or it might even mean programming the client to leave notes reminding himself/herself to practice. The environment must be changed so that the probability of regular practicing is increased.

If the client has reported that the new arrangements are satisfactory and still fails to carry out regular practicing (this may be evident either through self-report or through failure to evidence progress in the sessions; see Chapter 10), the therapist should try to detect a failure in the relaxation procedure which may be responsible for the client's lack of enthusiasm. If the client can achieve deep and satisfying relaxation in the office sessions, he/she should be willing to attempt to produce the same state at home. The therapist must insure that deep relaxation is occurring in the office; if it is not, the therapist's training procedure must be improved.

If the client continues to fail to practice even after a suitable practice situation has been arranged and relaxation has been achieved in the session, the therapist should tell the client, for example, "We will not be pro-

ceeding to the more efficient relaxation techniques until we get the early stages mastered, until we have evidence that you are practicing these procedures as they need to be practiced."

If the client continues to fail to practice, after the environment has been set up to facilitate such practice, after the procedures themselves have been made maximally efficient, and after a contingency such as that outlined above has been presented, this lack of cooperativeness may need to be discussed in the context of other problems; and the frequency of practice of relaxation may serve at a later time to indicate client cooperativeness in general.

WORDS AND PHRASES TO AVOID

As we noted in Chapter 6, the therapist should determine through the questioning after the first relaxation training session the things he/she is saying which affect the client's ability to become relaxed. The therapist should also get some indication of what the client feels is happening as relaxation occurs and use these feelings as part of subsequent relaxation "patter." The therapist should also learn which words or phrases are incompatible with relaxation. Besides whatever information is gathered from the client, however, we feel that there are certain words and phrases which should be avoided in any relaxation session, simply because they are likely to produce negative feelings in a significant number of people.

References to an already present physical weakness or defect should be eliminated. For example, if a client is noticeably overweight, the therapist should avoid statements like "Noticing the feelings in the muscles as they become heavier." References to sagging or drooping muscles should also be avoided in such cases. Such statements are likely to strike especially sensitive chords when used in connection with the muscles of the neck, abdomen, and face.

In general the therapist should use his/her own judgment; it is best to delete any reference which might possibly cause the client anxiety or embarrassment.

There are many possible alternative words and phrases which can be used (see Appendix B), and the risks associated with upsetting a client are too great to employ "loaded" statements. For example, in the case of facial muscles, rather than saying "loosening up," the therapist can say, "smoothing out."

The therapist should also avoid saying anything to the client which would imply that the relaxation procedures could produce any physical harm. Thus the therapist should avoid making statements like "O.K., tense these muscles hard and tight now, tense them to the breaking point," or "Tense the muscles until they feel like they could snap." Also, the therapist should not ask the client to "strain" his/her muscles, but rather to tense them.

A FINAL WORD ABOUT PROBLEMS

Whatever difficulties present themselves during a particular relaxation session, one cardinal principle should never be violated: the client should leave the therapist's office feeling better than when he/she entered it. If upsetting material is to be discussed in a session, it should be discussed prior to, not following, the relaxation training segment of that session. Of course, minor problems in the relaxation procedure can be discussed immediately after relaxation. However, it should be understood that following a good relaxation session the client is usually in a state of calmness and well-being which lasts for some time after the session itself is over. The therapist does not want to disrupt this feeling, and sessions should be planned so the disturbing material is presented before relaxation procedures. If, immediately after a training session, a client begins to bring up a "loaded" topic, the therapist is wise to remind the client that, since time is limited, this would be very good material with which to open the next interview. (Of course, if the subject brought up by the client is something that the therapist has been wanting to discuss for a long time, the therapist may prefer to violate the rule stated above. This should, however, be a rare exception.) Relaxation training should be the very last, very pleasant activity which takes place during the client's session with the therapist.

10   Assessing a Client's Progress

In this brief chapter we would like to discuss factors which indicate that appropriate progress in relaxation training is being made. These suggestions are supplements to, not substitutions for, the therapist's clinical skill at determining, for example, whether information given by the client is accurate.

REPORTS AND QUESTIONS FROM THE CLIENT

The therapist should look for spontaneous reports from the client that relaxation begins whenever the reclining position is assumed. This indicates that the environmental stimuli associated with relaxation have begun to control that behavior. As training progresses, the therapist should feel that he/she is almost wasting time toward the end of a given session, since the client should appear completely relaxed throughout the body even before all muscle groups have been relaxed. Reports from the client should substantiate this: "It seemed like an effort to tense the muscles of my legs because they were so deeply relaxed already."

Other indicators of increasing skill are statements by the client that he/she is in general feeling more relaxed even when the relaxation procedure is not being practiced. On an everyday basis the client should feel generally less aroused and upset. Of course, if such statements do not come from the client spontaneously, the therapist should feel free to explore these areas as training progresses. Normally, however, a rapidly improving client will provide such information prior to specific inquiry, or in response to some very general question such as "How are things going?"

Another indication of increasing skill which, unfortunately, might be misinterpreted as lack of enthusiasm, is an inquiry by the client as to whether the second practice session each day is still really necessary. The therapist should determine that the reason that the client is asking is that the skill is so well developed that the second practice session has become superfluous. In general, it is better to have the client continue "two-a-day" practicing until the counting procedure has been instituted. A bit of overlearning is not likely to be harmful and can help in application of the procedure to various tension-producing real-life settings.

INDICATIONS DURING RELAXATION SESSIONS

An important indicator of progress is the amount of time spent in each session. The aim of relaxation training is not to set speed records, but, if all is going well, the procedures used in the office would take progressively less time. If, after three or four sessions, the client is still giving frequent signals of failure to gain deep relaxation or is signaling other kinds of problems, the therapist should have some suspicions about the client's reports of regular practice.

Increasing skill will also result in less movement during relaxation. The client should ultimately, without actually being asleep, resemble a peacefully sleeping person. In addition, the client's breathing should slow down markedly over the course of any session.

Indications of the presence of deep relaxation in a client are such things as a "slack jaw." While a client may start a session with his/her mouth closed, toward the end of later sessions, the face should be very relaxed and the lips may part. The position of the feet also indicates degree of relaxation. They may move from being parallel to one another until they turn away from each other at about 45 degrees. This is something to look for in any session, and it can be expected to occur earlier in each session if good progress is being made.

If the client is not making appropriate progress, the therapist should carefully delineate the problem impeding progress and institute procedures designed to correct the situation.

11   Hypnosis, Drugs, and Relaxation

This brief discussion of hypnosis and drugs as they are related to relaxation training is included for two reasons. First, the therapist should understand the nature of progressive relaxation and be aware of both the similarities and the differences between such relaxation and that produced by drugs and hypnosis. Secondly, clients frequently ask questions regarding these matters. Since hypnosis is a well-known technique, clients often see similarities between popular notions of hypnosis and what they experience in relaxation training. Unfortunately, the misinformation and mysticism commonly associated with the hypnotist can be an obstacle to effective training. The client may fear that he/she will reveal personal information, will not remember events taking place during sessions, or will be made to do embarrassing things. Consequently, the therapist should be able to communicate to the questioning client an understanding of the difference between the two techniques and their effects. The current popularity of drugs can similarly affect client attitudes. Some clients become impatient with the time and effort required in training, and question why the therapist doesn't simply prescribe a tranquilizer.

THE NATURE OF RELAXATION

Relaxation training has been found to reduce subjective tension and affect a variety of other physiological processes. One may then ask how it is possible that the tensing and releasing of various skeletal muscle groups, combined with indirect suggestions, can result in changes in other bodily systems. Research has as yet produced few answers to this question. Past theories of "emotion" have interrelated voluntary muscle activity, internal autonomic activity, and mental behavior in numerous ways, placing primary importance on one or another. Current thinking emphasizes the role of the *reticular formation* (a diffuse nervous tissue located in the central nervous system) in mediating the interaction among

these three aspects. This is a model we can use to understand relaxation effects. Decreased autonomic arousal could in this way be caused by the things a person consciously thinks (*cognition*) and through decreased skeletal activity. Similarly, subjective feelings of anxiety may be eliminated by indirect suggestions or removal of the autonomic and skeletal components of those feelings.

A therapist need not accept this model in order to use progressive relaxation procedures; whatever framework is appropriate for a given client should be used. Whether it is the physiological relaxation or the "good" feeling accompanying relaxation that produces beneficial results, research indicates that benefits do occur in terms of lowered physiological arousal and subjective stress.

HYPNOSIS

Because of the "magic" surrounding the phenomenon of hypnosis, there is a current uncertainty as to its nature. Some researchers feel that it is a special psychological state and that they have data to support the claim. Other more skeptical investigators dismiss it as nothing more than intensive role-playing or attention-focusing. Regardless of its true nature, there are aspects of hypnotic procedures which are similar to features of relaxation training. Consequently, it is important to discuss the differences between them in order to eliminate from progressive relaxation both the connotations and the disputes that have surrounded hypnotism.

As Paul (1969a) has pointed out, hypnotic and relaxation procedures have at least seven common characteristics: (1) limited sensory intake, (2) limited body activity, (3) restricted attention, (4) deliberately monotonous stimulation, (5) altered body awareness, (6) closed eyes of subject, and (7) administration of motivational instructions. Both procedures aim at focusing the client's attention on certain bodily and psychological experiences. The primary difference between the two techniques is in the method of producing those experiences. In progressive relaxation training, the bodily sensations are produced through tension and release of the client's muscle groups.

Other contrasting features of progressive relaxation include the following: (1) Suggestions of relaxation, warmth, and the like are indirect and used only to focus the client's attention on what is "really" happening to the level of muscular arousal. (2) The skill is acquired through a learning experience over which the client has control. (3) The goal of progressive relaxation is simply to have the client become relaxed with focused attention; rarely does the hypnotherapist induce a trance for the sake of inducing a trance.

Of course, it should be noted that hypnosis and relaxation training have been used, singly and in combination, in both psychotherapy research and clinical practice. Indeed, both can produce the desired effects of subjective pleasantness, focused attention, and lowered physiological arousal. There are three reasons for preferring progressive relaxation over hypnosis in cases requiring tension reduction. First, as already mentioned, hypnosis carries with it undesirable connotations. Secondly, relaxation is something that a client can practice, become expert in, and use in everyday life. Finally, there is sound research evidence that relaxation training produces better results in terms of decreased physiological activity.

As mentioned earlier, Paul (1969a) compared the effectiveness of hypnosis, relaxation training, and a self-relax control. Twenty female college students were treated in each group. The results indicated that both hypnotic suggestion and relaxation training decreased both subjective tension and physiological arousal significantly more effectively than the control procedure. However, relaxation training was more effective than hypnotic suggestion in producing general physiological reductions earlier and in reducing heart rate and muscle tension.

DRUGS

There are two issues to discuss with respect to drugs.

First, anxious clients for whom relaxation training is indicated may already be taking some type of tranquilizing agent. Secondly, some therapists use drugs as a supplement to, or most often as a substitute for, relaxation training.

It is very surprising how little is actually known about the effects of drugs on human physiology and learning. Most research has been done on other species, and generalization of results is on weak ground. Furthermore, only recently have well-controlled research designs been employed in the area of psychopharmacology. This leads us to view drug usage quite conservatively, and we are not alone in this view (e.g. Reed, 1966; Jacobson, 1964).

During the first assessment interview, if it seems that relaxation training may be indicated, the therapist should ask whether the client is taking any form of drug. Further, the client should be asked to discontinue the use of any such drugs prior to initiation of relaxation training. (A thorough medical examination and, in some cases, withdrawal of the drug under medical supervision is generally advisable.) Very little is known about the effectiveness of any relaxation skills learned under the influence of the various drugs which are currently routinely prescribed. Since relaxation is a learned skill, it is difficult to say whether the learning will occur effectively in the presence of drugs and whether the learned skill will generalize to the nondrugged state if the client terminates drug usage after therapy. Therefore, it is best to eliminate the use of drugs prior to initiating relaxation training.

A variety of drugs have been utilized in behavior therapy programs. Wolpe, for instance, has used drugs, such as chlorpromazine, codeine, and meprobamate, in *in vivo* desensitization procedures. Various other agents have also been used to facilitate relaxation, either in systematic desensitization programs or in preparation for carrying out therapy programs.

There are four problems with these drug procedures. First, persons not medically trained cannot use drugs in therapy. Yet nearly any professional, or even nonprofessional, can, by the use of this manual, teach progressive relaxation. Second, research on the use of drugs in behavior therapy has been exclusively on the uncontrolled case study level. Thus, few generally applicable causative conclusions have been reached. Third, there is the problem of generalization of learning from the drugged to the nondrugged state. Some controlled research with other species has indicated loss of learned behavior when the drugs were removed. Finally, most applications of drugs have involved fast-acting agents used only within therapy programs of deconditioning.

They do not apply to long-term, client-controlled relaxation. A client could be drugged to such an extent that general relaxation results; however, the cost in terms of money, health, lost efficiency in performance, etc. is great. Relaxation is a skill that can be learned and used for the sake of tension elimination and subjective comfort without having to depend on anything beyond the client's own systematically programmed behavior.

Appendix A

tensing strategies are determined where needed)

III. Additional Instructions

    A. Various muscle groups are going to be compared with one another in terms of depth of relaxation.

    B. Release tension immediately upon cue rather than gradually.

    C. Once a group of muscles is relaxed, do not move it unnecessarily (except to make yourself comfortable).

D. Do not talk to me during this session. When I ask for a signal, please lift the little finger of the hand closest to me.

E. Notification of length of session and invitation to visit rest room

F. Removal of constraining items such as watches, rings, eyeglasses, contact lenses, and shoes

G. Questions and comments

H. Client reclines in chair

I. Explanation of dimming of lights

Appendix B

RELAXATION PATTER

The material which follows is suggested for use after the therapist has said the word "Relax." Do not attempt to use *all* of these statements after each tension-release cycle, since this would violate timing rules. Rather, a sampling of them in nearly any combination may be employed after any given cycle such that the therapist's behavior does not become routine and predictable.

". . .and relax, letting all the tension go, focusing on these muscles as they just relax completely, noticing what it feels like as the muscles become more and more relaxed, focusing all your attention on the feelings associated with relaxation flowing into these muscles; just enjoying the pleasant feelings of relaxation, as the muscles go on relaxing more and more deeply, more and more completely. There's nothing for you to do but focus your attention on the very pleasant feelings of relaxation flowing into this area. Just noticing what it's like as the muscles become more and more deeply relaxed; just enjoying the feelings in the muscles as they loosen up, smooth out, unwind, and relax more and more deeply. Just experiencing the sensations of deep, complete relaxation flowing into these muscles; more and more deeply and completely relaxed. Just letting them go, thinking about nothing but the very pleasant feelings of relaxation. Just let those muscles go and notice how they feel now as compared to before. Notice how those muscles feel when so completely relaxed. Pay attention only to the sensations of relaxation as the relaxation process takes place. Calm, peaceful and relaxed."

References

Bendig, A. W. Pittsburgh scale of social extraversion-introversion and emotionality. *Journal of Psychology*, 1962, *53*, 199-210.

Bernstein, D. A. Problems in fear assessment in outcome research. Paper presented at meeting of Western Psychological Association, Los Angeles, April 1970.

Bernstein, D. A. Behavioral fear assessment: anxiety or artifact? In H. Adams and P. Unikel (Eds.), *Issues and Trends in Behavior Therapy*. Springfield, Illinois: Charles C. Thomas, 1973.

Borkovec, T.D. Effects of expectancy on the outcome of systematic desensitization and implosive treatments for analogue anxiety. *Behavior Therapy*, 1972, *3*, 29-40.

Borkovec, T. D. and Fowles, D. C. A controlled investigation of the effects of progressive and hypnotic relaxation on insomnia. *Journal of Abnormal Psychology*, 1973, in press.

Campbell, D. T. and Stanley, J. C. *Experimental and Quasi-Experimental Designs for Research*. Chicago: McNally, 1963.

Cooke, G. Evaluation of the efficacy of the components of reciprocal inhibition psychotherapy. *Journal of Abnormal Psychology*, 1968, *75*, 464-467.

Davison, G. C. Systematic desensitization as a counter-conditioning process. *Journal of Abnormal Psychology*, 1968, *73*, 91-99.

Eisenman, R. Critique of "Treatment of insomnia by relaxation training": Relaxation training, Rogerian therapy, or demand characteristics.
Journal of Abnormal Psychology, 1970, *75*, 315-316.

Folkins, C. H., Evans, K. L., Opton, E. M., and Lazarus, R. S. Desensitization and the experimental reduction of threat. *Journal of Abnormal Psychology*, 1968, *73*, 100-113.

Geer, J. H. and Katkin, E. S. Treatment of insomnia using a variant of systematic desensitization: A case report. *Journal of Abnormal Psychology*, 1966, *71*, 161-164.

Graziano, A. M. and Kean, J. E. Programmed relaxation and reciprocal inhibition with psychotic children. *Behaviour Research and Therapy,* 1968*, 6*, 433-437.

Husek, T. R. and Alexander, S. The effectiveness of the Anxiety Differential in examination situations. *Educational and Psychological Measurement*, 1963, *23*, 309-318.

Jacobson, E. *You Must Relax*. New York: McGraw-Hill, 1934.

Jacobson, E. *Progressive Relaxation*. Chicago: University of Chicago Press, 1938.

Jacobson, E. *Anxiety and Tension Control*. Philadelphia: Lippincott, 1964.

Johnson, D. T. and Spielberger, C. D. The effects of relaxation training and the passage of time on measures of state- and trait- anxiety. *Journal of Clinical Psychology*, 1968, *24*, 20-23.

Johnson, S. M. and Sechrest, L. Comparison of desensitization and progressive relaxation in treating test anxiety. *Journal of Consulting and Clinical Psychology*, 1968, *32*, 280-286.

Kahn, M., Baker, B. L., and Weiss, J. Treatment of insomnia by relaxation training. *Journal of Abnormal Psychology*, 1968, *73*, 556-558.

Lang, P. J. and Lazovik, A. D. Experimental desensitization of a phobia. *Journal of Abnormal and Social Psychology*, 1963, *66*, 519-525.

Lang, P. J., Lazovik, A. D., and Reynolds, D. J. Desensitization, suggestibility, and pseudotherapy. *Journal of Abnormal Psychology*, 1965, *70*, 395-402.

Laxer, R. M., Quarter, J., Kooman, A., and Walker, K. Systematic desensitization and relaxation of high-test-anxious secondary school students. *Journal of Counseling Psychology*, 1969, *16*, 446-451.

Laxer, R. M. and Walker, K. Counterconditioning versus relaxation in the desensitization of test anxiety. *Journal of Counseling Psychology,* 1970, *17*, 431-436.

Lomont, J. F. and Edwards, T. E. The role of relaxation in systematic desensitization. *Behaviour Research and Therapy*, 1967, *3*, 11-25.

Paul, G. L. *Insight vs. Desensitization in Psychotherapy*. Stanford: Stanford University Press, 1966.

Paul, G. L. Physiological effects of relaxation training and hypnotic suggestion. *Journal of Abnormal Psychology*, 1969, *74*, 425-437. (a)

Paul, G. L. Extraversion, emotionality, and physiological response to relaxation training and hypnotic suggestion. *International Journal of Clinical and Experimental Hypnosis*, 1969, *17*, 89-98. (b)

Paul, G. L. Inhibition of physiological response to stressful imagery by relaxation training and hypnotically suggested relaxation. *Behaviour Research and Therapy*, 1969, *7*, 249-256. (c)

Paul, G. L. and Trimble, R. W. Recorded vs. "live" relaxation training and hypnotic suggestion: Comparative effectiveness for reducing physiological arousal and inhibiting stress response. *Behavior Therapy*, 1970, *1*, 285-302.

Rachman, S. Studies in desensitization I: The separate effects of relaxation and desensitization. *Behaviour Research and Therapy*, 1965, *3*, 245-251.

Rachman, S. The role of muscular relaxation in desensitization therapy. *Behaviour Research and Therapy*, 1968, *6*, 233.

Reed, J. L. Comments on the use of methohexitone sodium as a means of inducing relaxation. *Behaviour Research and Therapy*, 1966, *4*, 323.

Steinmark, S. W. and Borkovec, T. D. Assessment of active and placebo treatment of moderate insomnia under demand and counter-demand conditions. Midwestern Psychological Association, Chicago, 1973.

Straughan, J. and Dufort, W. H. Task difficulty, relaxation, and anxiety level during verbal learning and recall. *Journal of Abnormal Psychology*, 1969, *74*, 621-624.

Wolpe, J. *Psychotherapy by Reciprocal Inhibition*. Stanford: Stanford University Press, 1958.

Zeisset, R. M. Desensitization and relaxation in the modification of psychiatric patients' interview behavior. *Journal of Abnormal Psychology*, 1968, *73*, 18-24.